A Ragged Mountain Press
WOMAN'S GUIDE

CANOEING

LAURIE GULLION

Series Editor, Molly Mulhern Gross

RAGGED MOUNTAIN PRESS / McGRAW-HILL

Camden, Maine • New York • San Francisco • Washington, D.C. • Auckland • Bogotá
Caracas • Lisbon • Lon   Milan • Montreal
New Delhi • Sa   • Tokyo • Toronto

Look for these other Ragged Mountain Press Woman's Guides

• •

DEDICATION

To my parents, Torry and Bruce Gullion, for a childhood
that nurtured a love of the outdoors and canoeing

Ragged Mountain Press

A Division of The **McGraw-Hill** *Companies*

10 9 8 7 6 5 4 3 2 1

Copyright © 1999 by Laurie Gullion

Library of Congress Cataloging-in-Publication Data
Gullion, Laurie.
    Canoeing/Laurie Gullion.
       p.   cm —(A Ragged Mountain Press woman's guide)
    Includes bibliographical references (p.   ) and index.
    ISBN 0-07-025199-1 (alk. paper)
    1. Canoes and canoeing. 2. Boating for women. I. Title.
    II. Series.
  GV783.G724 1999
  797.1'22'082—dc21
                       98-41574
                       CIP

Questions regarding the content of this book
should be addressed to
  Ragged Mountain Press
  P.O. Box 220, Camden, ME 04843
  www.raggedmountainpress.com

Questions regarding the ordering of this book
should be addressed to
  The McGraw-Hill Companies
  Customer Service Department
  P.O. Box 547, Blacklick, OH 43004
  Retail customers: 1-800-262-4729
  Bookstores: 1-800-722-4726

Printed by Quebecor Printing Company, Fairfield, PA
Edited by Molly Mulhern Gross and Connie Burt
Design by Carol Inouye, Inkstone Communications Design
Project management by Janet Robbins
Page layout by Shannon Thomas
Illustrations by Elayne Sears

Photographs by Doug Hayward unless otherwise noted: page 128 (bottom), courtesy Jim Abel; page 24, courtesy Garrett Conover; page 33, courtesy Scott Gibson; pages 9, 11, 101 (all), 110, 119, and 124, courtesy Laurie Gullion; pages 27, and 71 (top), courtesy Cliff Leight; pages 13 (inset), and 128 (top), courtesy Bruce Lindwall; page 15, courtesy Michael Lyle; page 106, courtesy Alison Meader; page 37, courtesy John Meader; page 19, courtesy Mystic Seaport Museum; page 25, courtesy Nantahala Outdoor Center; page 23 (bottom), courtesy of Helen Peppe; page 26, courtesy Gigi Rioux; pages 13 (top), 17, 40, 59, 121 (top), and 131, courtesy Scott Underhill; and page 20, courtesy of University of Minnesota Press.

Special thanks to the canoeing specialists who loaned their talents for the photoshoot: Cathy Piffath, Jackie Peppe, Irene Yocz and Joanna Fernald. Thanks to Shelley Johnson at Powerface for the loan of the canoes and trailer. Thanks to Jim Dugan, photographer's assistant, and jack of all trades. Also special thanks to the town of Poland, ME, for permission to use the locations on Tripp Lake, and Upper and Middle Range Ponds. Thanks to Barefoot Beach, Sabbathday Lake, ME.

Scotchguard and Kevlar are registered trademarks.

"My father, Bill Mason, taught me that a canoe trip, be it an afternoon paddle or an expedition north of 60 degrees is not a race. Nor is it another check mark on a 'rivers-to-do' list. It's a journey. A journey of looking and listening and learning. A journey of discovery. And like him I find that canoeing can take you on a voyage of creativity, where stored experiences are there to treasure for a lifetime."

—Becky Mason

Foreword

"**N**ow what do we do?" I shouted across to the trip leader.

"Just follow the river." She could just as easily have told me to fly to the moon, for all I comprehended, but in the folly of youth my partner and I started off, clueless as to the requirements of whitewater or its dangers. I was 13 years old, on my first canoe trip, sitting in the stern of a loaded aluminum canoe, hovering at the top of a stream just turning from flat- to whitewater.

On our way down that short run, 50 feet or less, I bet, we passed the crumpled form of the canoe that took off just before us, and as we passed it—rapidly, for we had no idea how to slow ourselves—I remember thinking "Oh my, how'd that happen ? . . ."

We navigated that small section of rapids by sheer luck. I have no idea what the trip leader was thinking, taking novice canoeists down that drop. It wasn't that *my* experience was so bad—we just pointed the canoe and let the river take us—but the vision of that crumpled aluminum boat, and my friends in the water, made me leery of canoeing. Oh, I can get in a boat, paddle in the bow, and even occasionally take the stern and try to keep her in a straight line. (I like to blame the weaving course the canoe makes when I'm in the stern on the unbalanced way that my heavier bow partner sits in the boat.) See chapter 5 for Laurie's explanation of how to paddle straight! But since that frightening sight, I've been reluctant to explore the possibilities of seeing the world by canoe. I've let what I saw on that trip, and the unanswered question posed (What should they have done to prevent crashing?) stop me from canoeing. But the advice—and wisdom—offered in *Canoeing: A Woman's Guide* provides a way for reluctant canoeists like myself to get back out there.

The book in your hands offers the support and knowledge you need to paddle your own canoe confidently, on still or fast water. Here you'll find lots of practical advice about getting started, finding the right instructor, and moving beyond your first paddle. *Canoeing: A Woman's Guide* is based on the increasingly popular all-woman clinics and instructional classes, and the information is presented in a manner that respects how women learn and grow.

What's so different about the way women learn? If you're like me, you want to hear a description or overview of a move or tactic before launching into it. I guess you could say I'm a fan of the "talk-it-over-and-think-it-through-first" school of learning. I like to know how to avoid big rocks in the river *before* I'm asked to canoe down whitewater (see page 111). I want to know if a canoe is the right type for me before I sit in it (see pages 43 and 90 for Laurie's descriptions of the types of canoes available). I want to hear advice from someone who is like me, someone I know and trust. And I benefit from learning in a group because I hear other folks' questions—and discover I'm not the only one wondering just why my canoe won't go straight (see chapter 5)! This learning style builds knowledge one step at a time: as our comfort level increases, so does our ability to tackle the new skills. We've done our best to mimic these learning conditions in The Ragged Mountain Press Woman's Guides. *Canoeing: A Woman's Guide* provides solutions, advice, and stories from women who have paddled lakes and rivers near and far, women who have overcome the nagging fears and self doubts that often accompany us at the start of any adventure.

I hope Laurie's words and the approach used in this book help get you out canoeing, by yourself or with a friend.

I'll look for you out there.

When you get a break from your adventures, drop us a note to tell us how we're doing and how we can improve these guides to best suit you and your learning style.

MOLLY MULHERN GROSS
Series Editor, The Ragged Mountain Press Woman's Guides
Camden, Maine
January 1999

An avid outdoorswoman, Molly Mulhern Gross enjoys running, hiking, camping, sea kayaking, telemark skiing, in-line skating, and biking and has just started snowboarding. She is Director of Editing, Design, and Production at Ragged Mountain Press and International Marine.

CONTENTS

CONTENTS

Acknowledgments

Canoeing people are a special kind, willing to tell endless stories and share their Big Moments in canoeing without much prodding! I'm grateful for the many wonderful conversations, the written reflections, the unsolicited videotapes, and the phone calls from women who had just one more thought! The following people made this writing project one of the most enjoyable I've ever undertaken:

The many women who returned my canoeing surveys, especially those who felt constrained by the small spaces and sent long letters instead. Your love for canoeing is obvious.

The Norway Four: Kathie Armstrong for telling me in no uncertain terms what this book's content should be; Reed Asher for nailing me about the preponderance of men I quoted in my Norway story in *Canoe & Kayak*; Linda Jones for funny references about "The Men and Laurie"; and serene Jean McIntyre for not bugging me about anything! Thanks for shaping my thoughts during that wonderful Nordreisa journey when I was writing this book in my head.

Paddling pal Mary McClintock for many provocative opinions expressed about what shape my writing should take; for a willingness, perhaps even a fondness, for paddling upriver against current to reduce end-of-the-day stress; for ginger scones!

The photo session folks who looked graceful against gale-force winds: Cathy Piffath and Jackie Peppe of L.L. Bean's Outdoor Discovery Program; Joanna Fernald, whose Arctic Barrens canoeing form still rocks; and Irene Yocz for just being lovely Irene!

The women in the 1997–98 and 1998–99 Outdoor Leadership Program at Greenfield Community College in Massachusetts for sharing their apprehensions about canoeing and being cheerful guinea pigs in my canoeing laboratory.

The careful and amenable crew at Ragged Mountain Press: Molly Mulhern Gross for shaping a vision with this series; Janet Robbins for her calm presence; photographer Doug Hayward for his helpful knowledge of paddling. And thanks to Shelley Johnson for going first in the series and sharing her manuscript.

The archivists at Mystic Seaport in Connecticut and Smith and Wellesley Colleges for help in tracking historical sources. A special thanks to my favorite researcher, Dick Winslow, for the almost weekly packet of information—particularly the illuminating articles about women paddlers from old or obscure journals. Also my mother Torry Gullion and uncle George Hughes for exploring that whole new world of electronic cataloguing to chase canoe club information.

My husband Bruce Lindwall for his unending patience and humor during a spring of dueling laptops, distracted conversations, and canoeing-technique discussions while he was trying to finish his dissertation.

Chapter 1

GREAT BEGINNINGS

A North Woods cabin for a canoe getaway.

I can still see the tiny log cabin as clearly as the narrow brook that runs past its front porch, although I have not returned to that special corner of the North Maine Woods in 17 years. In my childhood, the logging company abandoned a nearby access road, and when the bridges crumbled, my family had to hike several miles in to the old hunting and fishing camp with food and gear packed in ash baskets. My sister and I at 9 and 12 years old found the excursion fraught with intense excitement. Wild woods and wild animals—it might as well have been a canoeing expedition to the Arctic wilderness in our young minds.

With our cousins, we were given boundaries in which to roam the fork between quieter Benson Brook and deeper, more dangerous Ship Pond Stream. And explore we did. I felt like the ancient cartographer who penned "Here be dragons" at the edge of a map of the known world. The dark, northern forest yielded many discoveries thrilling to suburban kids—rare, yellow lady's slippers in a damp patch by the brook; the abrupt tail slap of a beaver whose lodge dominated a small bog; a young, startled deer that bounded away from us into the brush.

Lady's slipper.

When I think of the freedom given us by our parents to travel alone in the woods, I marvel at their confidence in our abilities to take care of ourselves. Then, as an adult, I look at a map and realize that our triangle of freedom stretched just over a square mile! Small enough for a margin of safety to reassure parents, yet large enough for me to indulge my Nancy Drew fantasies and believe I was having a wonderful, slightly dangerous adventure.

EXPLORING NEW PLACES

Farther up the trail lay two ponds, and tucked into the bushes by the shore of Little Benson Pond was a woodstrip canoe built by a local craftsman. No roads led to the pond, so we hiked into the seclusion of it, sometimes carrying a second canoe. A canoeing excursion with my family meant many things, and quietness wasn't always one of them. We laughed like loons and listened to the echo return across the water. The eerie sound of the real bird was a rare thing in the 1960s and special when we heard it. We explored inlets, rustling through the thick alders lining the shore to find mushrooms and wildflowers under the trees. The quietness I do remember was the slip of a narrow wooden paddle into clear, cold water while I stared at the pond bottom, unable to figure out the depth—mesmerized even then by the rhythm of the strokes.

My memories are rich with the color, texture, and smell of the water, woods, and sky. I've realized that these early outdoor experiences in which canoeing played a prominent role encouraged a vital awareness of my surrounding environment. Our trips on Little Benson Pond are my earliest images of paddling—deep in the woods without seeing another person—and they have shaped my participation for the past 35 years. Canoeing has continued to be a means to explore new, distant places—and my favorite destinations are those with few people.

In 1980, I had the opportunity to travel by canoe above the Arctic Circle to the Northwest Territories of Canada, and I quit my job as a newspaper reporter to do it. I knew little about the northern tundra, but I was intrigued by the personal commitment required to spend six weeks canoeing in one of the last and largest wildernesses in the world. No escape, once the float planes dropped off our group of 21 people. I knew

"The dark, northern forest yielded many discoveries thrilling to suburban kids— rare, yellow lady's slippers in a damp patch by the brook; the abrupt tail slap of a beaver whose lodge dominated a small bog; a young, startled deer that bounded away from us into the brush."

how to canoe in whitewater, having learned in college, but I questioned whether I could physically endure the hardship of the weather and the daily mileage. Traveling the Elk, Thelon, Dubawnt, and Kazan rivers also would require paddling upriver and portaging over heights of land to enter new drainages.

THE EXPLORATION WITHIN

I wasn't in the best of condition, and I'd never camped outdoors longer than a week prior to this journey. Six weeks! Could I handle it mentally, especially the dynamics of a large group? What would my parents think about my abandoning full-time employment? I was blessed with qualified support from my family. Not unqualified, because I think my parents suffered the conflicting emotions of apprehension and excitement about their daughter seeking such a challenge. But they always had supported my need to pursue some unorthodox interests, recognizing, as my mother once characterized me, that I have been "determined since birth." With my family intrigued by this jump into a real wilderness, I prepared to paddle 1,100 miles across the Arctic.

A canoeist explores the Nahanni River of sub-Arctic Canada.

This profound experience was a major milestone in my life, for I discovered that I could handle the rigors of wilderness canoeing. When we paddled into the native village of Baker Lake at our journey's end, the community opened its school to us for an overnight stay. The 12 women on the trip took turns checking out new muscles in the bathroom mirror, grinning at the physical changes after six weeks of paddling, and clowning around with naked poses that profiled our wiry backs. The guys in the men's room were more restrained, we learned later, but we women were taking unabashed pride in our strong bodies.

• •

"**P**erhaps it is the intensity and simplicity of my emotional reaction to the canoeing experience that continues to lure me to explore new lakes and rivers. I don't completely understand what drives me to heed the water's call. I just know that I continue to arrange my life so that I can spend more days gliding across water in a canoe."

• •

What about the emotional impact? At 26 years old, the experience gave me such self-confidence that I proceeded to develop my own outdoor instructional business and to write "how-to" books about paddling and skiing for the next 14 years. Risk-taking behaviors take many forms, and an entrepreneurial approach to employment was a natural extension of the decision-making skills I had learned in that remote environment. I returned to co-lead four trips to Canada's North as part of the Arctic Barrens Expedition program, introducing many beginners to the wonders of completing a two-month canoeing journey in the stark but enthralling tundra.

At 40 years old, during a midlife crisis that I was determined NOT to have but suffered anyway, I accepted a full-time educational administration job at the University of Massachusetts! Wasn't I supposed to be "moving up" in life? Recently, I left that position to return to outdoor instruction and writing, for I have learned that my heart lies in sharing my outdoor experiences with other people, in helping them to explore the outdoors at a level that challenges them. This book is a part of that goal.

> "There are valleys unpeopled and still.
> There's a land that beckons and beckons
> And I want to go back and I will."
>
> —Robert Service, *In the Spell of the Yukon*

THE LURE OF CANOEING

It's water that continues to lure me. I recently stumbled across some favorite lines by Canadian poet Robert Service, the Bard of the North, that resonated once again.

Canoeing can be viewed as a journey measured in miles, compass directions, schedules, and classifications of river difficulty, where these ingredients create a certain character to each lake and river trip. What is more interesting is whether the experience leaves me and my companions serene, unsettled, thrilled, tired, or rewarded. Perhaps it is the intensity and simplicity of my emotional reaction to the canoeing experience that continues to lure me to explore new lakes and rivers. I don't completely understand what drives me to heed the water's call. I just know that I continue to arrange my life so that I can spend more days gliding across water in a canoe.

It doesn't always have to be in an unpeopled wilderness. I can paddle in nearby Barton Cove to watch nesting bald eagles or watch the sun rise over my favorite stretch of the Connecticut River, just a quarter-mile from my rural Massachusetts home. Canoeing allows me to feel supremely alive, more intensely aware of my environment—and that's worth sharing with other people.

Chapter 2

THE FEMALE CANOEIST

Women have traveled in canoes for thousands of years, following water trails long before the more recent late nineteenth-century popularity of recreational canoeing for ladies. The indigenous cultures of North America, Greenland, and the former Soviet Union used the skins of seal, walrus, and caribou around wooden frames to create the *umiak* or canoe. In some cultures such as the Greenland Inuit, the umiak came to be defined as the women's boat because it handled the transport of family groups to new settlements. This large, undecked skin boat of 25 to 40 feet could be paddled, rowed, or sailed long distances. The more stable umiaks were used occasionally for hunting large mammals such as whales, but men usually used the shorter, highly maneuverable kayak for hunting.

As a circumpolar mode of transportation, umiaks are believed to be the oldest working boat in the world. Petroglyphs in Norway from 3000 B.C. show illustrations of what some archaeologists believe to be open skin boats, although this opinion is controversial. Nonetheless, umiaks are undoubtedly ancient craft that have played a crucial role in global migration. Asian peoples prized their seaworthiness in traveling to the New World, and Polynesian cultures used outriggers on canoes to explore thousands of miles of the South Pacific. Cultures worldwide copied the functional, symmetrical design, using whatever native materials allowed a boat to float—logs, bark, reeds, or animal skins. The canoe has been a boat for all peoples.

Canoe travel lured many to local waterways.

MODERN CANOEING FOR WOMEN

Canoeing as a modern recreational activity began around 1850 in the Peterborough region of Ontario in Canada. Craftsmen began to develop plank-style canoes, which by the end of the century led to an explosion in building boats at a more affordable price, welcomed by the general public. English barrister John MacGregor also returned to Europe with a sail-fitted oak canoe that he propelled with a double-bladed paddle similar to the one used today by kayakers. MacGregor recorded his exploits in 1866 in the popular *A Thousand Miles in the Rob Roy Canoe on the Rivers and Lakes of Europe*, which fueled an amazing rise in canoe travel for pleasure on both continents.

Victorian attitudes that treated recreation as a frivolous activity waned during this time, and the canoe became a popular vehicle for cruising, camping, and courting. It was considered an acceptable activity for women in North America and Europe. Ladies' periodicals such as *Cosmopolitan* began to applaud the virtues of canoeing in glowing articles like "Canoeing in America," published in the October 1893 issue. Fashionable vacation travel now expanded beyond the more tame seaside and mountain resorts to remote waterways for a real adventure.

Reading old issues of the magazine is a fascinating experience because they chronicle the change in social norms for women and exercise. No longer viewed as harmful to women and an impediment to childbearing, exercise was touted as beneficial to general good health. Activities such as gymnastics, basketball, bicycling, tennis, and golf now were considered acceptable (although still somewhat suspect if performed vigorously); *Cosmopolitan* described canoeing as "natural exercise and delightful recreation." Women's colleges like Smith and Wellesley added canoeing to their curricula. Canoeing logs from Smith College's physical-education department show a century's worth of commitment to national standards in the activity and the development of independent women. One instructor suggested that girls taking out canoes must have passed the college's paddling test, even if with a date!

Still, some magazine readers felt that canoeing should happen with men firmly in control because glossy advertisements from canoeing manufacturers and travel organizations largely featured women in the bow of canoes. Sometimes the need for a woman to even take a stroke appeared unnecessary, for they seemed to be more bow ornament than paddler! The July 1903 issue of *Sail and Sweep* magazine included, beneath a picture of a woman being paddled in a canoe, a lovely ditty that begins "A sweet little maid. . . ."

Urban canoe clubs abounded at the turn of the century, with thousands of members, regattas for the general public, races for men, and the construction of ornate boathouses that still house some clubs today. The American Canoe Association yearbooks show a special category of "honorary" or nonvoting membership for women during that time. (They weren't allowed full governing membership until 1944, according to Ronald Hoffman's *History of the American Canoe Association, 1880–1960*.) The idea of "manless canoeing" was still a novel idea in some quarters, and concerns about the nature of women's involvement continued to surface in the literature.

"**A** sweet little maid with hair like night,
And eyes of the self-same hue
Reclining at ease, with charming grace,
'Gainst the [thwart] of my canoe."
—*Sail and Sweep* magazine, July 1903

The January 1905 edition of *Sail and Sweep* profiled singer Jessie Bartlett Davis as an ardent outdoorswoman who fished and hunted for partridge and deer in (gasp) the breeches of a man. Author Edgar Guest expressed admiration cloaked in surprise that she "handled the frail [canoe] with the skill of an Indian," negotiating a rapid "as if she had spent all her life on water." This praise was high indeed in an era that romanticized the American Indian and complimented competent female paddlers as "squaws" or "princesses." However, a woman still had to observe certain social boundaries. Mr. Guest felt compelled to note that "there is nothing of the Tom Boy or hoyden about her . . . no member of the party ever forgets that Mrs. Davis is a woman."

I wonder what Mr. Guest would have thought of Mina Hubbard, a 35-year-old widow who canoed across the uncharted Labrador peninsula from east to west in 1905, the first white traveler to complete such an arduous traverse with native guides. A deeper and darker story exists behind

The lounging canoe. (Mystic Seaport)

• •

"**Y**ou're not just learning to paddle. You're creating a whole new world to discover."

—Ruth Jones, owner, Kittatinny Outfitters

• •

her remarkable journey—she succeeded in this goal, whereas her husband had died of starvation two years earlier. In *A Woman's Way through Unknown Labrador*, Mrs. Hubbard fiercely recounts how she vindicated her husband's reputation by completing his dream, yet she devotes few words to the immensity of her undertaking in a cold and inhospitable land. (See this listing in chapter 11, "Resources.")

The truth is that adventurous women were canoeing in wildly remote places even though some, like Ruth Terborg's father, still saw wilderness as "no country for women." Ruth wrote in the 1936–1937 *Appalachia* that her father, an annual visitor to Timagami in Ontario, questioned whether women could handle "long unmarked portages, big headwinds and black flies, canoe partners (who) didn't speak to each other for weeks." Undaunted, she and her three sisters only "longed for more of this exciting and forbidden country" after learning to canoe on the Raquette River in New York's Adirondacks. With advice from *Woodcraft for Women*, they constructed a tent, purchased "bifurcated garments" that "dressed each knee separately," and wielded the axes they'd had little opportunity to use on previous trips with men. Ruth's story is an amusing account of four well-prepared women paddling two 80-pound canoes that were "200 in the air" and "18 feet long underfoot (40 feet long, I swear, overhead)." The light tone is a sharp departure from male accounts of similar experiences during the same period, for I can't imagine men laughing over naming a favorite island Mt. Ararat and their tent the Ark (it never leaked a trickle)—and admitting it in writing!

Women helped create the modern canoeing industry in the United States and continue to play crucial roles at all levels. They are presidents or executive directors of national paddling organizations, like Janet Zeller of the American Canoe Association, Rebecca Wodder of American Rivers, and Heidi Krantz of Professional Paddlesports Association (these are all listed in chapter 11). Some, like Kay Henry of Mad River Canoes, own manufacturing companies. Others operate the most respected paddling schools in their country, like Bunny Johns, president of the Nantahala Outdoor Center in North Carolina, and Claudia Kerckhoff-Van Wijk of Madawaska Kanu Camp in Ontario. Other related enterprises must be added in, such as the magazine industry, where Judy Harrison, with her husband Dave, started *Canoe & Kayak* magazine.

An early pioneer is Justine Kerfoot, now in her 90s, who operated Gunflint Lodge in Minnesota on a dirt track that has become one of the main roads into the Boundary

JUSTINE KERFOOT

W O M A N OF THE
BOUNDARY WATERS

WITH A NEW AFTERWORD BY THE AUTHOR

CANOEING, GUIDING, MUSHING, AND SURVIVING

FOREWORD BY LES BLACKLOCK

Women have written about their canoeing trips since the late 1800s. Here, Justine Kerfoot.

Waters Canoe Area. Purchased by Justine's mother as a fishing lodge during the Depression, the business expanded to canoeing and guiding to make the operation more versatile. In *Rivers Running Free: Canoeing Stories by Adventurous Women*, Justine writes about learning to be a stern paddler:

> *This new art served me well, for in the struggle to pay our bills, I worked into a guiding routine of paddling a canoe-load of guests the 16 miles (including four rapids and eight portages) to Saganaga Lake and picking up a return group to go back the 6 miles to Gunflint Lodge via two rapids, a portage, and across Sea Gull Lake, where we were met by the lodge truck. At times, as I heaved a heavy canvas-covered canoe onto my shoulders at a portage making this round trip, I thought, "There must be an easier way than this to make a living."*

Despite the hardships, Justine is vividly aware of her surroundings, and her love affair with this harsh and demanding land is evident in the essay and in her autobiography, *Woman of the Boundary Waters: Canoeing, Guiding, Mushing, and Surviving*. A passion for the landscape is a common thread in my conversations with many women about why they paddle, and it only intensifies through the years. The connection to the river continues to inspire businesswomen like Ruth Jones, owner of Kittatinny Outfitters in Pennsylvania, who rents 1,000 canoes and 400 campsites, employs 200 people, and manages seven outposts along 120 miles in the Delaware Water Gap. An only child of parents who started the company nearly 60 years ago, Ruth grew up along the river and says she was "born to be a paddler. . . . Any day on the river is a good day!"

Ruth still thrills to see eagles, beaver, and other wildlife, always scanning the shoreline to explore that interesting link between river and land. She said, "You're not just learning to paddle. You're creating a whole new world to discover." Ruth operates one of the largest outfitting companies in the United States, yet she sets a goal to paddle 200 miles a year on her days off because she needs to be on the river. Does she reach her goal? Absolutely.

The Delaware's beautiful ledges and surrounding forests make it a popular river, and Ruth believes her company has a responsibility to use the natural resources wisely. For the past decade, Kittatinny has organized annual river cleanups that have won it awards from the National Park Service and the White House. "You just can't keep taking from the resources. We earn our livelihood from it, and we have to take care of it," she said.

WHO CANOES TODAY?

Today the waterways are afloat with women. The popularity of paddlesports in general has exploded in the last decade with 24.8 million people who canoe, kayak, or raft, according to the 1996 National Survey on Recreation and the Environment. The majority are canoeists, where participation totals 14.1 million—and of those 14.1 million canoeists, 5.34 million are women. Canoeing is believed to happen in a family context quite often. *Canoe & Kayak* has 230,000 North

American readers, and 69 percent of the readership is married. The reader's average age is 42, with the largest number of readers in the 35-to-44-year-old category.

Marion Stoddart, owner of Outdoor Vacations for Women Over 40, runs many trips that offer canoeing as one of the activities, and she sees a big difference in women's participation in the last 15 years. "When I started, many women had to ask their husbands' permission to participate," she said. "Then they had to ask for the money to pay for the trip." But those barriers no longer exist. She thinks that more women have jobs that provide them with funds and decision-making power, and the social climate has changed. Now it's more acceptable for older women to be involved in outdoor activities, including canoeing.

TYPES OF CANOEING

Canoeing is an activity with many themes, once you've learned the basic strokes and maneuvers. The place to begin is with *flatwater canoeing,* which enables you to paddle the calm water of lakes and rivers. Here you learn to control your canoe without the added variable of current, although you will learn how to deal with wind. Flatwater canoeing allows a comfortable introduction, and you'll be able to feel exactly what your strokes are doing to move the canoe.

Once you've learned basic boat-control skills, then you may choose to explore some interesting variations on flatwater canoeing, which are explained in the following sections. You also may learn how to adapt your flatwater skills to the intrigue of *whitewater canoeing.* Here you begin to explore moving water in rivers, where the current begins to speed up and flow around and over obstacles such as rocks to create interesting river features. You'll learn tactics for handling the push of current against the canoe.

Two types of paddlers exist in all types of canoeing: *solo* (one person) and *tandem* (two people). A solo canoeist sits near the middle of the boat to better control both ends. Tandem canoeing divides responsibilities in the canoe between the *bow* (front) and the *stern* (back) paddler. Solo canoeing allows you to be independent, which in today's busy world means you don't have to track down a partner to paddle. While initially a little frustrating, solo canoeing is ultimately extremely rewarding because you know who is making the boat behave.

Tandem canoeing has its own joys and frustrations! It's extremely social, and many like the additional power of two people propelling the canoe. Generally, the bow paddler sets the tempo, while the stern paddler keeps the boat on track and matches the bow paddler's pace. Tandem canoeing also requires cooperation and clear communication, particularly in whitewater situations. Some of my finest paddling experiences have been with partners with whom the chemistry is perfect. Then tandem canoeing is the sweetest, cooperative experience. I can't begin to explain the mystery of why it works with some people and not with others—people who may be extremely gifted paddlers and lovely women, too! Just accept the reality that some tandem partnerships are not meant to be and hope that the lack of boat chemistry doesn't apply to your live-in partner!

The strokes and maneuvers that you learn with the help of this book will enable you to explore a wealth of canoeing opportunities. Here are some possibilities for continuing participation.

Freestyle canoeing

Imagine a style of canoeing similar to figure skating that mixes technical paddling moves with creative self-expression. Think of smooth, flowing maneuvers set to music with judges grading both technical and artistic merit. Freestyle canoeing is a flatwater activity that enthusiasts describe as "a dance on water"—a paddling ballet that is fun for spectators to watch. Dramatic boat leans combined with slow-motion maneuvers test the paddler's balance and precision; as the sport evolves, women are introducing more dynamic elements, such as gymnastic stunts, into their routines.

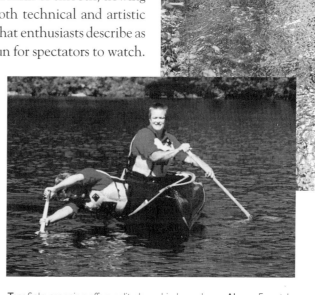

Karen Knight, the reigning national solo champion, says freestyle is "the art and science of canoeing" where precise, controlled moves are combined with relaxed, expressive ones. Of course, she thrilled the crowd in 1996 by executing a split in the curved *side* of her canoe, leaning the boat dramatically without flipping over and setting the record for the highest solo paddler's score ever. At just under 5 feet tall, Karen's

Top: Solo canoeing offers solitude and independence. **Above:** Freestyle champion Karen Knight and Jackie Peppe have added drama to the sport.

gymnastic background has helped her raise the level of competition to new athletic heights. She also introduced faster music and routines to what had been a slower style of competition.

Freestyle canoeing is popular and accessible, because you only need a small patch of water, a liking for dance, and a willingness to risk a few swims when practicing the extreme boat leans characteristic of the sport. The sport uses some new terms to describe the same old canoeing moves, but it's easy to speak the language quickly. Karen, who teaches for L.L. Bean's Outdoor Discovery Schools, recommends an instructional lesson to learn the basics of technique; then supplement with your own imagination to create a unique water ballet. Competitive events for women include solo and tandem competition, and they are particularly popular in regions with ponds and flatwater rivers among people who don't need the thrill of whitewater.

Maine Guide Alexandra Conover poles precisely upriver and down.

Traditional canoeing and poling

Watching Maine Guide Alexandra Conover maneuver a long wood-and-canvas canoe three times her size with a narrow paddle is a delightful experience. Put a 12-foot wood pole in her hands to push off the lake bottom, and the canoe tracks just as straight. Alexandra brings a grace and athleticism to canoe-poling that allows her to slide downriver effortlessly, standing up in her canoe to pole amid the rocks. She also can pole upriver, jumping up through chutes of water with precise maneuvering of her pole and nimble balance.

Canoe-poling can be the ultimate low-water activity in summer and fall, allowing you to explore shallow streams without worrying about a car shuttle. Just put in, start poling upstream, and earn the reward of an easy return trip down the river to the car. Skilled canoe-polers can handle the thrills of big, bouncing whitewater, although the standing position does encourage a few fast ejections if you strike an unforeseen obstacle! Once you've learned river maneuvers with a paddle, you can substitute the pole and accomplish the same moves.

Alexandra founded North Woods Ways in Maine with her husband Garrett in 1980, and they have guided thousands of people using traditional methods and equipment. She loves poling because it allows the same "careful, clean style of canoeing" that she pursues with a paddle. Alexandra also likes to explore little-seen locations that lack road access: "I can pole upriver and explore the tributaries to major rivers that we guide on. These areas are otherwise inaccessible. There's incredible freedom to go upriver and down."

Another Maine poler, equity stage manager Lisa Bragdon, likes poling "because of what a powerful tool it is for me. I'm small—5'2" on a good day with the wind blowing right! Poling allows me to control a boat like a fish in the water."

"I can pole upriver and explore the tributaries to major rivers that we guide on. These areas are otherwise inaccessible. There's incredible freedom to go upriver and down."

—Alexandra Conover, Maine Guide and owner of North Woods Ways

Canoe slalom

Women's Olympic slalom events are available only to kayakers, but recreational canoe slalom attracts devoted followers in regions of the United States where special race series exist. Canoeists negotiate a 25-gate course suspended over stretches of whitewater rapids 300 to 600 meters long. Women in solo, tandem, or mixed (man/woman) classes attempt to negotiate as quickly as possible a series of hanging poles called *gates* in designated upstream- or downstream-facing positions. The canoeists try to complete the course without accruing penalties from touching poles (two seconds) or missing gates (50 seconds).

Nantahala Outdoor Center president Bunny Johns continues to compete.

Paddlers take two runs down the course; both runs are added together for the final score. The challenge is to be fast and clean through the gates in frothy whitewater, which creates an exciting spectator sport at technically difficult points along the course. Canoe slalom is an intriguing challenge for the paddler because it requires that you be very precise in your moves. A body built or trained for sprinting is helpful, too! The race lasts only three to four minutes. Regional and national championships are scheduled each year.

Marathon canoe racing

Marathon canoe racing offers a lively mix of events and distances, where paddlers can race from 5 miles (8 km) to ultra-distances of 250 miles. The most common race distance is 7 to 15 miles, which can take one to three hours. Women and girls can enter a variety of classes, including juniors, masters (40 years and older), women, families, aluminum canoes, and plastic canoes; they also can choose from solo or tandem categories. The diversity of opportunity lets women select a level of competition tailored to their desires, which is why marathon canoeing is so popular. Regional and national championships are held each year.

The emphasis is straight-ahead speed in long narrow boats designed to track well. The site is usually calm water, and the race might require one or more *portages* (carries around dams). The appeal for me is the Zen-like trance possible in open stretches resulting from repeated rhythmic strokes. Marathon races require stamina and a mindset that lets you keep your own pace while staring at the backsides of other paddlers! Many races have mass starts, so all classes leave the starting line at the same time. The top women can find themselves in a dogfight for position in the front of the pack. Knowing how to handle the wakes from faster boats is an asset. I rather enjoy the sociability in the back, where people talk and apologize when they veer too close!

A canoe leg can be added to a triathlon too, which is a nice variation on the usual run-swim-bike theme. Because I can't swim well, the run-bike-paddle events suit me nicely. Good canoe teams are in hot demand on the triathlon circuit because the canoeing portion can be the weakest leg for many teams. In the spring, a whitewater leg may be the choice.

Whitewater downriver racing

These events are a variation on canoe marathons and can be nearly as long. Racers need to descend rapids and avoid obstacles in the whitewater, so a higher degree of skill is needed to compete—or at least the ability to make fast route-finding decisions while jockeying for position among other boats. Canoes are often started individually, about a minute or so apart, to avoid congestion in the difficult sections of whitewater. These competitions are as much about a paddler's strategy on whitewater as they are about her conditioning. Some races do involve big crashing water, where the challenge is staying dry in the heart of the drops. Races can last about 20 minutes or longer, which makes the sport a more aerobic activity than slalom.

Whitewater rodeo

Rodeo is another great emerging spectator sport, where competitors execute a series of difficult moves in a river playspot characterized by waves and *holes*, which are depressions below rocks or ledges where the river rolls back on itself! Spectators delight in seeing competitors spin around on waves, cartwheel end over end, and nail the perfect pirouette—the wilder the ride, the better for the competitor and the crowd. Getting flushed out of the hole is considered poor form!

Currently, women compete against men in the canoe rodeo events, since the sport is in its infancy. Quebec's Ghyslaine "Gigi" Rioux placed fifth among 25 competitors at the 1998 World Rodeo Championships, which featured only one other woman in canoeing. Gigi had been steeped in the Canadian tradition of canoe camping, but three years ago she turned to the wildness of rodeo. She likes the purity of the challenge: "I love working with the water. The water has laws, and if you don't follow them, it just doesn't work."

Maneuvers get scored on artistry and degree of difficulty, so you need technical skills, a flair for the dramatic, and comfort in places that resemble washing machines. Highly sought characteristics are retentiveness, meaning whether the paddler stayed in the hole, and verticality of the canoe, which is pretty exciting to see. Rodeo has a great vocabulary of moves as well. A *retendo* is an end-over-end flip that lands you back in the hole, but then you progress to the following: McTwist, whippet, bow wing over, a river-bashing McChicken, a McChicken with Mayo (a smile during the bashing), and more. I'll leave it to you to explore the meaning behind the names.

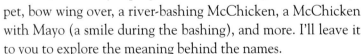

"The water has laws, and if you don't follow them, it just doesn't work."
—Ghyslaine "Gigi" Rioux, 1998 World Rodeo Champion

Playing in frothy holes lures canoeists to rodeo.

This canoeing book is designed for women who have wanted to paddle meandering streams in wonderful places, who are intrigued by the rush of dancing water, and who seek the feelings of accomplishment that come from learning to skillfully handle a canoe. Whether you are a newcomer to canoeing or already have traveled with a paddle in hand, this book will help you experience the activity in new and rewarding ways.

The history of women and canoeing is an ancient one—from the animal-skin boats called *umiaks* paddled by Inuit women of the Arctic North to early wilderness travel by pioneering women in long skirts and bonnets. I draw on the stories of women past and present to help you understand essential canoeing skills; through this wealth of women's voices, I hope you can appreciate and experience what has lured women to canoes for hundreds of years.

"The canoe and the paddle are beautiful objects, graceful in repose," writes Kathie Armstrong, who has canoed for more than 60 years, many of them in New York's Adirondack Park. "When united by a paddler, the whole becomes a dance; the water provides the music and sets the rhythm. To participate in this dance and follow the music is an art and a privilege."

Canoeing as a dance is a theme that repeatedly surfaces in women's writings and conversation—from the slower rhythm of a misty morning paddle to the quicker tempo of a stormy lake or river. Drifting with the current is an opportunity to become absorbed in the rhythms of the river. Others describe canoeing as a kind of poetry or artistry—an intensely creative process.

Becky Mason, 34, of Chelsea, Quebec, said: "[A] fascination I have with canoeing is the artistry of combining and utilizing the infinite number of strokes effectively. I grew up watching my dad, Bill Mason, canoeing—be it rapids or flatwater he loved it all. One of the wonderful memories I have is seeing my Dad launching from our dock alone in his old Chestnut on the glassy, flat, calm waters of Meech Lake and making his canoe dance a beautiful language. As I

"The canoe and the paddle are beautiful objects, graceful in repose. When united by a paddler, the whole becomes a dance; the water provides the music and sets the rhythm. To participate in this dance and follow the music is an art and a privilege."

—Kathie Armstrong, canoeist for more than 60 years, New York grew older and gained more paddling skills, I would go out with my own canoe and join him in the dance."

Although it never came to fruition, one of her father's last projects was a film on canoe ballet for the National Film Board of Canada. Becky practiced long hours to perfect her technique and the fluid movements needed for the film, tentatively entitled *The Magic Paddle*. In 1987, her father retired from filmmaking before the film was brought to final production, but he encouraged her to continue sharing the art of canoe ballet, and her Classic Solo Canoeing program was born.

"I find that canoeing is not a separate entity in my life but part of my psyche and personal makeup, as it was with my Dad. He was always so busy and active, working and going non-stop for months at a time. But he recognized that he really needed the quiet solitude of a wilderness journey to nourish his soul and rekindle his spirit, and this he passed on to me. He also showed me that the best way to experience this was in a canoe. He taught me that a canoe trip, be it an afternoon paddle or an expedition north of 60 degrees is not a race. Nor is it another check mark on a 'rivers-to-do' list. It's a journey. A journey of looking and listening and learning. A journey of discovery. And like him, I find that canoeing can take you on a voyage of creativity, where stored experiences are there to treasure for a lifetime."

What I discovered this past year is that a woman's passion for canoeing is intimately linked with an appreciation for the natural world. Many women wrote vividly of childhood experiences at summer camp or on early family trips—the words crisp and colorful as if the experiences happened just yesterday. That connectedness to the land, water, and sky has motivated them to continue canoeing in new places that give an unobstructed view of the natural world. Kathie Armstrong wrote, "Standing on an esker, overlooking the vast scheme of life around us, we felt our insignificance and yet we were empowered. . . . Each journey expanded our skills, self-reliance, and love of wilderness. Our trips grew longer and farther from home."

The connectedness can begin at an early age. Hannah Roebuck, 10, who attended the 1998 Wilderness Canoeing Symposium at the Hulbert Outdoor Center in Vermont, has grown up in a canoe with her parents. She said quite simply why she loves canoeing: "For the sound of the paddle in the water, and walking on land!"

Like Becky Mason's connection with her father, a woman's involvement is often grounded in experiences with other people—with children, parents, partners, and friends. Some have received canoes as wedding presents, and many happily paddle with spouses; others vow never to paddle again with their partners, but they have found others with whom the chemistry in a canoe works just fine! Alison Meader, a Maine Guide who produced a *Babes in the Woods* video about introducing small children to extended canoe camping, says, "Never let anyone push you into running whitewater you don't *want* to run. My husband and I have a rule that has worked for over 15 years. Never try to goad or shame the other into running whitewater you really don't want to run." Each person should be allowed to make her own decision to run or not run a rapid without interference from group members.

Women are united in how powerful a shared canoeing experience can be. Their mentors are often the familiar people who introduced them to the activity—fathers who also taught them to fish, a friend who offered a simple, quiet getaway on the river; husbands who wanted company in the canoe. They describe these inspirational canoeists in many ways—often enthusiastic, patient, and supportive people whose paddling is graceful and elegant. One thing is certain: If you begin to canoe, you will find your own canoeing family, related or not, who will be ready to lure you on The Next Trip.

ABOUT THIS BOOK

To help you follow your own canoe "music," I share with you the skills and techniques to safely paddle a canoe on calm water and whitewater, the knowledge to purchase your own equipment, the ability to plan an enjoyable trip in new locations with family and friends, and my enthusiasm for emerging activities such as freestyle canoe ballet and whitewater rodeo. Most importantly, I hope that you enjoy your initial dance with a canoe, for the rewards are many and varied.

In writing of her many wilderness canoeing trips in places from Canada to Norway, Kathie Armstrong said, "Traveling for many days taught us to focus in the present—the movement of the paddle, the rapid around the bend, the reflection of the clouds, the cry of the peregrine falcon— nothing more, nothing less than the moment at hand. Often, there was a great unexplainable sense of joy."

In this book, you will meet many women like Kathie for whom canoeing has brought much joy. I hope that their stories inspire you as a canoeist and that you build not only a repertoire of useful skills, but also a wonderful collection of paddling experiences and stories. Through these stories, you can share your experiences with other newcomers to the activity in a manner that will encourage them to pursue the rewards of canoeing. The ripple from your canoe strokes and stories will grow ever wider.

Kathie Armstrong

Chapter 3

⚓ GETTING STARTED

In our canoeing dreams, we see ourselves paddling effortlessly across smooth water, the splash of porpoises on the horizon and stately pines reflected against a golden setting sun. In reality, those first few strokes are best taken under the watchful eyes of more experienced people who can offer thoughtful advice and a large measure of safety in the event that a rising wind destroys the reverie! You want your first canoeing strokes to be positive ones, and it's especially important if you've talked family members or friends into trying the activity with you!

Many Americans think they were born with a canoeing gene in their DNA because this Native American sport is a dominant part of our heritage. But I've found that women are very open to asking for assistance in learning to paddle because they want to paddle well. Often, friends and family question our desire to take canoe lessons, puzzling over why summer camp learning isn't enough. Canoe lessons? Isn't that an oxymoron?!

Well, learning to canoe efficiently takes knowledge and practice, and it's here that women excel. My best students have been patient women who learn to finesse their strokes rather than grunt their way through maneuvers. Thoughtful in our learning and willing to listen, we have learned to "paddle smart" and can be the most technically proficient paddlers in a canoe lesson.

The value of instruction is clear, as you'll hear from these women who reflected on their own beginnings in canoeing:

Demonstrating paddle techniques.

- "Get instruction. When I started the whitewater program for the Schenectady Chapter of the Adirondack Mountain Club, I sent survey forms to many people (members or not) who had done some whitewater. The most succinct reply to the 'How did you learn whitewater?' question was 'trial and error' with error underlined." Betty Lou Bailey, 68, retired mechanical engineer, Schenectady, New York

- "Take a beginning/starter paddling day with a parks and recreation department with a woman friend . . . talk with the instructors to check out their style of teaching (supportive versus yelling!)." Becky Roehrs, 39, IBM manager, Raleigh, North Carolina

- "Take formal instruction from a good, supportive instructor. Don't try to canoe with your partner/spouse when you are both just learning how! Very stressful on a relationship." Mary McClintock, 40, freelance researcher, Conway, Massachusetts

- "Go with safe people you trust or take a clinic eventually to learn good technique. If you feel safer in single-gender groups, find access to these—they do exist." Lisa Carter, 39, educator, Newland, North Carolina

- "Try solo rather than tandem—take lessons." Judy Halstead, 45, physical chemistry and environmental studies professor, Saratoga Springs, New York

Many women were fortunate to learn canoeing as young girls with their families, in Girl Scouts, or at summer camp. They speak movingly of clearly remembered first trips from 50 years ago. Others arrived at the activity later in life, like one Quebec woman who experienced a midlife crisis, was separated from her husband, and bought a canoe for solace. Some learned to paddle through college outing clubs. One woman paddled her first whitewater river at age 82, because "It was time to stop putting it off!"

Here are other suggestions from women who love canoeing:

- "Do what suits *you*, not what someone else tells you you should like." Marge Shepardson, 51, teacher, Marlborough, New Hampshire

- "Don't listen to the doubters . . . always carry your own load. Carry your own canoe." Jane Barron, 39, owner, Alder Stream Canvas outdoor gear, Durham, Maine

- "Find a friend who likes to do what you like and do it together. One or the other of you will be eager to pull the other away from everyday obligations." Ann Ingerson, 42, college teacher, Craftsbury, Vermont

- "No fear or shame in dumping—if you don't dump, you're probably not learning as much." Shauna Stuber, 42, transportation manager, Seattle, Washington

- "Play! Discover! Explore!" Paula Wanzer, 49, recreation therapist, Meredith, New Hampshire

COMMON CONCERNS

You may have specific concerns about canoeing that can affect how comfortable you are when learning to paddle. It's natural to be a little apprehensive when exploring a new activity. Make sure you get the answers that you need to be relaxed in your learning, because you'll progress faster and more enjoyably. If an instructor or agency doesn't take the time to address your concerns, then don't travel with them. There are plenty of places that can deliver reassurance and an excellent introductory experience.

It is risky to try something new like canoeing, but don't let your own head hold you back. Optician Marsha Withers, 45, of Richmond, Virginia, remembers her first canoe camping experience with her husband and another couple: "I was so nervous and afraid, but ended up loving it and wanting more. . . . I am very lucky that Jim and I share this passion and as a couple it has given us both great joy and excitement. . . . Canoeing is the first sport that I feel I can do well in."

Reed Asher, 56, a potter from Pawling, New York, has an interesting perspective on the impact of perceived risk on her early whitewater experiences. She remembers a river section with current sweeping around a bend against a cliff wall, then bouncing through waves toward a bridge abutment. "As a beginner, this looked terrifying, even though we had been instructed on exactly how to do it and had practiced the needed maneuvers. Needless to say, we all got through it just fine."

Reed continued, "I was even more scared the second time [when she returned to the river]. In my mind, the cliffs were huge, the force of the water tremendous, and the wave at the bottom . . . not to mention the bridge abutment being almost unavoidable. When we rounded the bend and saw that part of the river, the rock formations were small, the water not that fast, and the space between

Getting comfortable in the water can relax your learning.

· ·

"I am never so alive and focused
as when I'm in it up to the gunwales, and we are a team."

—Reed Asher, age 56

· ·

"Learning to paddle is learning
about rhythm, not power."

—Rebecca Barry, age 54

· ·

the wave and the abutment big enough to drive a truck through. The experience taught me how relative perceived risk is. The more skill you have, the more difficult the challenges that can be mastered. I am never so alive and focused as when I'm in it up to the gunwales, and we are a team."

Women share similar concerns about beginning to paddle—before a lesson, in telephone conversations with prospective students, I answer the same questions repeatedly. My message is that you'll find soul sisters in canoeing who may be just as nervous initially about being afloat. Don't let it stop you from getting the information you need to dive into the experience.

What if I can't swim?

It doesn't matter because you'll be wearing a life jacket that keeps you afloat in the unlikely but possible event of a capsize on flatwater. Lots of people with no or poor swimming ability participate in canoeing, and many paddle whitewater rapids, comfortable in the knowledge that the lifejacket keeps their head above water. Besides, if you worry about flipping over in the middle of the lake, it's guaranteed that you'll trip over the canoe getting out of it and fall in ankle-deep water near shore!

What if I get stuck in the boat or under it?

Even if you kneel in a canoe, you will float free of the seat and to the side of the canoe if you capsize—you will probably keep your hair dry as well! The lifejacket makes you bob right up. Some whitewater canoes have straps that run across the tops of your thighs when kneeling, which are designed to let you lean the canoe during river maneuvers. But your instructor will review how to easily come free of these straps, and you don't have to use them if you don't want to (they can be unbuckled).

What if I get too tired and can't finish?

Lots of adjustments can be made for stamina, and good planning can help. Make sure that your paddling or lesson group has breaks built into the schedule. Use the conditioning suggestions in chapter 10 before paddling to get ready. Embark on a short loop, rather than a point-to-point trip, so the trip schedule is more flexible and you can turn around at any time.

Rebecca Barry, 54, a court security officer from Haverhill, New Hampshire, says that "learning to paddle is learning about rhythm, not power." Remember, too, that good technique is more important than strength, and your skills will take you farther than you think. If you are worried about upper-body strength, you'll find that modern paddling technique makes it easier to use your total body, rather than just your arms. We review an approach in chapters 5 and 6 that encourages you to use the big muscles of your back and chest rather than your smaller arm muscles. You'll paddle more strongly as a result.

What if I hold other people back?

One of the best ways to learn is with women-only groups, where other women will share that concern. You'll find a very supportive group of patient people who are willing to take the time to learn the skills proficiently. Tandem canoeists may be concerned that they'll affect their partner's experience, but one of the joys of tandem paddling is developing a good communication system and working as a team. Your paddling skills and conditioning aren't big factors here; being open, flexible, and clear in communication are far more important. If you are still really worried about holding people back, take a private lesson first.

What if I can't pick up the canoe?

Canoes are a lot lighter these days because of new technologies, and there are some nifty techniques that allow you to lift a boat onto a car by yourself. But you should also free yourself of the notion that only one or two people should be able to carry the canoe to water. I gave up that masochistic approach when I injured my back about a decade ago, and the best part about paddling with a group is that everyone can help get the boats to shore. Personally, I like six-person carries! Explore some alternative carrying techniques in chapter 4 to make transport easier, and compare the qualities of canoes and other gear in chapter 8.

For an **overhead carry**, roll one end of the canoe overhead (1–3). Then walk backward slowly until the other end of the canoe lifts off the ground (4–6).

. . . .

"**F**ear was my biggest barrier. I haven't overcome it; I've just learned to manage it. Fear keeps you alive."

—Deborah Laun, age 37

. . . .

I'm feeling pretty fearful in general about this . . .

Deborah Laun, 37, an industrial designer from Syracuse, New York, shares these thoughts: "Fear was my biggest barrier. I haven't overcome it; I've just learned to manage it. Fear keeps you alive. Now, I ask myself: Will I be annoyed with myself later for wimping out on this? How bad are the consequences? Am I having fun if I do this? (Or can I do something else and have fun?) I tell myself I am here to have fun."

I've never been in the stern . . .

The best thing about women-only clinics is that someone has to get into the stern! And you're clearly not the only one intimidated by this position; I've watched many women graciously offer the seat to someone else. Somehow we accepted the idea of the "stern man" as the captain or director of the craft—the ultimate authority—which causes some apprehension. Think of canoeing as a cooperative venture, where the bow paddler actually initiates a lot of the moves because her end leads the way. It's absolutely essential in whitewater canoeing that the bow paddler make important decisions about the specific route because she can see the obstacles better. The stern paddler just follows her lead! Yes, the stern paddler has to keep the boat tracking straight on flatwater, and you will zigzag at first. Just stop trying to be perfect immediately, relax your white-knuckled clench on the paddle, and you'll learn just fine.

What if I lose my gear?

You can waterproof your gear so that it floats. The easiest way is to line your packs with a garbage bag, put all your gear inside the bag, twist the top of the bag like you're wringing out a towel, fold the twist over, and wrap an elastic band tightly around it. There's enough air in the bag to let your pack bob in the water. Always put the plastic bag inside the pack, so it doesn't snag and develop leaks.

Instruction with a reputable paddling school, outfitter, or club is the best place to begin. It will give you the confidence to take charge of your end of the canoe, including the stern. And it will give you the rescue support inherent in a group experience, which is the safest way to learn.

FRIENDLY CLUBS

If you want an inexpensive way to learn to paddle and a means to find some new friends, then local paddling clubs are the best option. Check with the American Canoe Association (ACA) for a list of paddling clubs in your area—you're likely to find a 100-year-old club with a venerable history and well-stocked boathouse, or a more recently organized institution that meets in members' homes or at local public sites (see chapter 11 for a list of paddlers' associations). What you are guaranteed to find is a great collection of local paddlers who are committed to sharing their sport with newcomers. You might find some great paddling characters as well.

Take Marge "River Mom" Cline of the Chicago Whitewater Association, for example. Marge has been paddling for 20 years, ever since her daughter's Girl Scout troop became interested in paddling trips. In her trademark cat-eye glasses and boldly colored warmup suits, Marge is well known nationally as a tireless supporter of youth paddling programs, winning the ACA's "Legends of Paddling" award. I first met her on the banks of Tennessee's Ocoee River at the 1987 National Open Boat Championships. She had driven other people's children to the competition, camped with them for a week, and chaperoned them down a few local rivers. Her daughter and son are long since grown and her husband has lost interest in paddling, but Marge continues to teach free paddling classes for her club. A certified ACA instructor and instructor trainer who loves freestyle canoeing on ponds, as well as whitewater excitement, she says, "Don't isolate me to one discipline. I like 'em all."

The River Mom believes in two basic rules for learning to canoe: "It's got to be safe and it's got to be fun." She recommends club instruction for the following reasons:

- **Safety.** Because it is unsafe to paddle alone, learning with an organized group gives you a big measure of physical security. Knowledgeable people will come to your rescue if you need it.

- **New Friends.** Club programs let you find a new circle of paddling friends whom you're going to trust with your life. You don't need to come with a partner; come alone, Marge invites, and you'll find one among the folks who are taking the lessons or club members who run lake and river outings.

Marge "River Mom" Cline teaches hundreds of club members.

- **Comfort.** People need to be emotionally comfortable in learning new skills, and you'll be in good company in a club program. The volunteers who are leading club activities could be doing lots of other things on weeknights or weekends rather than teaching classes in the local Y pool or pond, but they've chosen to teach you because they love it.

- **Affordability.** Club instruction is cheaper than commercial programs—if not free—once you've paid a membership fee. You also may find a collection of club-owned equipment that you can rent cheaply for future practice. Members, who usually become boat hounds, also bring their own craft, so you will be able to experience different types before you buy one.

THE OUTFITTER OPTION

You may want to combine your canoe learning with outdoor travel, particularly if you are vacationing with your family and you know they aren't interested in extended instruction. Signing on with an outfitter can get you the basic skills quickly with more time spent on the watery trail. Finding an outfitter is easy; the back pages of paddling magazines are filled with them, and a state tourism agency can provide you with a list servicing your dream area. But finding an outfitter who understands your needs will require a little more effort.

Heidi Krantz, president of the Professional Paddlesports Association, the trade organization for canoe liveries and outfitters, says that knowing the difference between a *canoe livery* and an *outfitter* can be helpful. A canoe livery (similar in concept to horse liveries of bygone years) usually provides a basic service, such as public boat rentals. An outfitter may be more likely to provide additional services, including trips and instruction.

Heidi thinks the livery/outfitter approach benefits newcomers to the activity for these reasons:

- **Variety.** If you are not sure if you'll like canoeing or if you'll last through a day-long lesson, then rent a canoe or take a short trip. Many companies let you get a taste of paddling with short-term rentals (one to two hours) or they offer trips from one hour to a half-day. A good rental agency will have a variety of craft—not just banged up aluminum canoes reminiscent of summer camp—so you can experience the joys of a light, maneuverable boat as well.

- **Access.** Liveries and outfitters are located on some of the nicest waterways in the United States, from intimate, clear streams to bouncy whitewater. Launch your boat easily and quickly right from their beach or dock. Particularly if you are vacationing in a new area, you might not find out about these gems unless you contact a local shop.

- **Easy Participation.** Let the company handle the logistics and take on the role of vacation planner. If you want a downriver trip rather than an out-and-back loop, they'll pick you up or shuttle your car to the end of the run.

- **Basic Instruction.** If you don't have paddling experience, a reputable outfitter will provide instruction appropriate to the river or lake and provide you with a basic safety orientation. More shops are using certified instructors these days, so you can obtain professional tips to get you sliding across the water quickly.

- **Customer Service.** Heidi says that association members treat customers like valued guests. "People go out of their way to be hospitable," she said, "because they take pride in keeping up strong connections with people."

You can contact the Professional Paddlesports Association for a list of liveries and outfitters across the United States and at selected locations in Canada. Checking with local chambers of commerce is also a useful strategy.

Here are some tips for selecting an outfitter:

- **Choose an agency that has existed for a few years.** It will have worked the bugs out of its operation by now. For the same reason, avoid any trips advertised as "New"! You don't want to discover with the staff that the "quaint" lodging is more rustic than advertised.

- **Examine your own goals and match them to the experience.** Trips range from completely supported, where vans transport your gear to the lodge and sauna waiting at day's end, to self-supported, where you carry your personal gear and a portion of the group gear. The first type can provide a nice initial experience to ease you into canoe camping; the second gives you a taste of freedom right away. Some trips may require that you perform some group chores, others make them optional or unnecessary (e.g., the trips where the staff delivers coffee to your tent door). However, expect to pay the price for this luxury.

- **Consider children.** If you're feeling a little cranky about traveling with children or hormonal adolescents, check the age restrictions imposed by the outfitter. Conversely, if you want a great trip with your kids, ask the outfitter about their experience with children. You can tell if they really like traveling with young paddlers. They may set restrictions, depending on the difficulty of the trip and the kids' paddling experience. Ask about equipment sized for children; it is available at some shops.

- **Know your limits but don't underestimate them.** A half-day experience may be the perfect introduction to the activity before a commitment to a multiday tour. Check the daily schedule to find out how many hours each day are devoted to paddling. If additional time for photography and hiking is important, a high-mileage trip (e.g., 10 to 20 miles a day on flatwater) is not for you. Nervous about your strength or endurance? A properly paced trip will have substantial meal, snack, and rest breaks built into the schedule, as well as a buffer for bad weather. A little unsure about those final two days of whitewater? Choose a milder trip first; it's always better to be a little relieved than scared witless, regardless of what your so-called friend says. Good friends understand and accept your need for a mellower introduction. A good outfitter also will interview you to make sure that your goals and background are suitable for the experience so that it's likely to be successful.

- **Ask for an equipment list.** A good outfitter will spell out clearly what the company will provide (usually all technical equipment such as boats, paddles, life jackets, tents, cooking gear, and first aid gear). You will be asked to provide all personal clothing from a specific checklist, which should be developed by the company for the specific environment and season. If they expect customers to use the same list for canoeing and backpacking, then don't trust them. Sleeping bags (and sometimes tents) are usually considered personal gear, which you must supply. Some but not all outfitters do rent these items. Check the life jacket to see if it's a comfortable, jacket-type vest rather than the old orange "horse collar" or around-the-neck vest, which is uncomfortable enough that most people just stash it in the canoe. The best jacket is one that is worn!

- **Clarify the total cost.** Check to see if a canoe rental is a per-person or per-boat cost; it's usually per canoe. However, a canoe trip is typically assessed as a per-person cost. If you and your two kids are renting a canoe, you can easily rent a kayak for the third person, which can make it a more interesting day for your kids. Check whether the outfitter will charge for use of specialized gear such as wetsuits, booties, and drybags. Some include it in the total package, particularly if it's part of an instructional program. If the trip involves international travel, the airfare may not be included in the advertised price. Ask about any hidden costs, such as entry fees to public and private lands or parking fees at riverside sites. Most outfitters are very up-front about this because they want customers to understand the recent charges levied by agencies such as the U.S. Forest Service.

- **Ask about discounts.** One might be available if you provide your own canoe, but few outfitters offer the fee reduction. They prefer that you use their boats, which they know are well equipped and repaired. Some trip shuttles may require the use of participant vehicles, and you may not want your tired old sedan bumping along a muddy access road. Some outfitters will reimburse mileage costs if you use your vehicle, but be sure to ask.

- **Check the proposed menus.** You may prefer basic foods to keep the trip cost low. But if you are paying a premium price for the experience, then the food better qualify as wilderness gourmet. The best thing about canoeing is that the boat carries the weight—unlike backpacking, where you do—so don't let the outfitter skimp here! Special diets usually can be accommodated with advance notice, and many companies produce outstanding vegetarian menus. Of course, if your idea of the perfect outdoor meal is a sizzling steak in the evening and bacon on the morning breeze, then ask if it's part of the deal.

- **Know the cancellation policy.** Expect to pay a sizable fee upon registration and the balance prior to the trip. After all, the outfitter has to calculate menus, boats, and staff in advance. Check the cancellation policy, because you may forfeit your deposit if you cancel within the no-penalty cancellation period before the trip. In the event of unforeseen emergencies, some companies will transfer your deposit to another trip—but don't expect it if it isn't stated. Be prepared to go if it rains; only potential safety hazards such as a thunderstorm or high winds are likely to force an outfitter to cancel a trip.

OUTFITTER CHECKLIST —AT A GLANCE

- Choose an agency that has existed for a few years.
- Examine your own goals and match them to the experience.
- Consider children.
- Know your limits but don't underestimate them.
- Ask for an equipment list.
- Clarify the total cost.
- Ask about discounts.
- Check the proposed menus.
- Know the cancellation policy.

Canoeing is a family affair.

• •

"**Y**ou can learn a lot from other people, by watching them, not just the instructor—especially if the instructor helps this happen."

—Bunny Johns, age 57
President of Nantahala Outdoor Center

• •

INSTRUCTIONAL SCHOOLS

The primary mission of paddling schools is to educate people about canoeing and kayaking, rather than guiding trips, and you can find the most in-depth technical instruction here. Schools offer a high level of professional instruction with staff who have taught a wide variety of students and can aid greatly your development. Check the back pages of *Canoe & Kayak* and *Paddler* magazines to find the school closest to you.

One of the most respected American paddling schools is the Nantahala Outdoor Center (NOC), established in 1972, the same year Burt Reynolds crashed down the Chattooga River in Georgia in the movie *Deliverance* and helped popularize the sport. President Bunny Johns, a national canoeing champion who, at 57, still beats women half her age in races, reflected on her own "trial and error" beginning. A former biology teacher, Bunny tried to teach herself to roll a kayak using a two-page pamphlet with stick figures, which resulted in months of failing to roll. "My learning experience was protracted, and I learned a lot of bad habits," she said, wryly.

A wonderful and insightful teacher, Bunny helped develop the ACA's instructional program nationwide. She said paddling schools can offer you these benefits:

- **Excellent Professional Instruction.** Trained instructors can help you learn the skills efficiently and quickly without bad habits. They employ a wealth of tasks, paddling imagery, and problem-solving skills that enable them to focus on your learning style, body type, and conditioning. You learn fast under these conditions. The best part is often the instructors' skill at analyzing technique, and they can offer clear feedback about your developing paddling style.

- **Enjoyable Groups.** Learning in a supportive group is "just plain fun," said Bunny. "You can learn a lot from other people, by watching them, not just the instructor—especially if the instructor helps this happen." In a structured format with supervised practice, including rescue practice, people learn how to make good decisions in challenging situations and to take responsibility for themselves.

- **Women-only Courses.** Extremely popular in recent years, these classes have proven to be a wonderful way for women to learn to paddle. Many women like the absence of what Bunny calls "female/male interactional stuff"! Women, who can tend to feel they are holding back the group, find that these classes reduce that pressure. Bunny believes that these classes progress just as far as a mixed-gender group—they just get there a different way. "There's lots of laughter and lots of support," she said.

- **The "Package" Approach.** Instructional schools often offer a total package, which includes instruction, meals, lodging, transportation, and all equipment. It's a no-fuss experience that can be a wonderful vacation. Especially when food and lodging are factored in, the course price becomes reasonable.

Bunny remains committed to instruction, still teaching two or three times a week in summer, despite overseeing all NOC operations. "I have to," she says simply.

Use the outfitter checklist as a guide for asking questions about an instructional school as well. Know before you go, and you'll have a wonderful introduction to your first canoeing experience.

Chapter 4

GETTING FRIENDLY WITH YOUR CANOE

Your learning will be helped by gaining some basic technical knowledge about canoeing. While the canoeing "language" can get quite arcane, I want to introduce simple terms to get you started. Communication is key in canoeing, especially between partners, and the simplest language is best. If confronted with a retail or rental clerk who talks in techno-babble (and canoeing does attract them), be willing to ask for a simple explanation. Heed the advice of instructor Marge Cline of the Chicago Whitewater Association: "Don't get lost in the nomenclature. You *can* paddle without knowing a lot of terms!"

> "**D**on't get lost in the nomenclature."
>
> —Marge Cline,
> Chicago Whitewater Association

In this chapter, you'll also learn some quick tips to get the boat to the water and begin canoeing. Carrying the canoe may seem daunting at first, but it can be easy. Kay Henry, owner of Mad River Canoe in Vermont, talks with a lot of women about the virtues of lighter canoes, but she also observed that a few simple handling techniques can help you get any boat from a car to water. "If you can show someone how to handle a boat out of the water, they think 'Oh, I can do this,'" Kay said.

For some women, it's important to handle the canoe alone, and today's lighter boats can certainly help. (Chapter 8 discusses different types of canoes available.) But if confronted with a 70-pound model, be willing to ask for some assistance. Many hands do make light work. No longer should you feel compelled to limit yourself to one or two people for carrying a canoe. I talked recently with a trip leader who said he has a rule that all carries must be solo to make good time. Consequently, the women never get a chance to portage a canoe on his trips. When I suggested that two, three, or four women could carry a canoe to offer the experience and satisfaction of completing a challenging task, his response was that it would undermine the schedule. The mischievous side of me suggested that the schedule could be changed to accommodate the learning of new skills! There's no need to buy into the message that it has to be done a certain way. Be flexible and creative in getting comfortable with handling your canoe.

NAMING THE CANOE

Amidships—the middle of the canoe

Beam—the widest part of the canoe; usually at or behind the boat's middle point

Bow—the front section of the canoe

Centerline—a line (usually imaginary) along the canoe's bottom, running from bow to stern; also called the keel line

Deckplates—plates at the bow and stern that attach to the gunwales and deflect water

Depth—the distance between the gunwales and the canoe bottom, measured at the centerline at the boat's deepest point

Draft—the distance between the waterline and the canoe bottom; the degree to which a canoe rests in the water

Gunwales—the rails along the edges of the hull

Hull—the main body of a canoe stripped of any parts

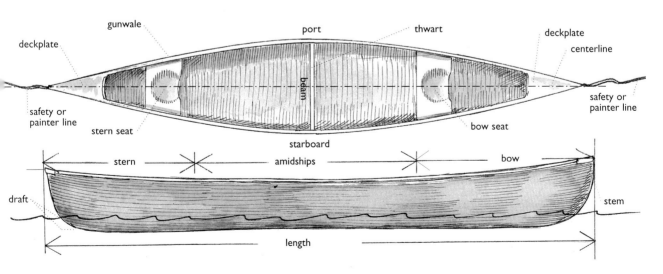

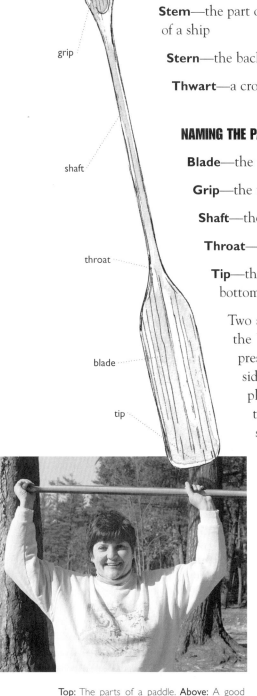

Painter lines—safety lines attached to the bow and stern

Stem—the part of the bow where the sides of the canoe meet, as on the prow of a ship

Stern—the back section of a canoe

Thwart—a crosspiece between gunwales that gives shape to the hull

NAMING THE PADDLE

Blade—the part of the canoe paddle that is placed in the water

Grip—the top of a paddle shaft, where the canoeist grabs the paddle

Shaft—the narrow neck on a paddle between the grip and the blade

Throat—the point at which the blade attaches to the shaft

Tip—the edge of the blade most likely to strike the lake or river bottom

Two additional terms can be helpful in learning strokes. Think of the blade as having a *powerface*, which is the side of the paddle pressed against the water during the forward stroke. The other side of the paddle is the *backface*. Some women spray-paint or place colored tape on one side of the paddle in order to consistently use the powerface; it helps simplify the learning of new strokes.

Holding the paddle properly

Keep a loose, relaxed grip on the paddle so you don't transmit any tension into your paddling. Clasp the grip firmly and maintain this clasp; don't swivel the grip in your palm because it can confuse your learning of the strokes. Hold the shaft with the other hand at a point that offers good leverage against the paddle. The best way to find the right spacing is to raise the paddle above your head and see if your arms form right angles at your elbows. If your "shaft" hand is holding the throat of the blade, then the paddle is too short and offers little leverage with strokes. Selecting and sizing a paddle is addressed in more detail in chapter 7, where I provide advice on purchasing your own gear.

Top: The parts of a paddle. **Above:** A good paddle grip creates right angles at the elbows.

THE IMPACT OF BOAT SHAPE

Each canoe has the same basic parts, but the overall shape of the boat can be modified for different types of canoeing. Here I present the two most basic boat shapes to get you oriented. The figure below shows a flatwater or *touring* canoe with a longer design that will allow it to track straighter in the water; the figure on the next page shows a whitewater or *multipurpose* boat suitable for many paddling environments. Additional variations to these basic shapes are addressed in chapter 8, where I present more in-depth information on a myriad of canoes.

Touring (flatwater) model

This flatwater touring model is a longer slender boat with a sharper bow and stern. The narrower bow shape, shown below, lets the canoe cut cleanly through the water. I think of the bow as a knife cutting through butter. However, the squarish *stem* prevents the canoe from turning easily, which aids in straight tracking. A longer length of 17 to 18 feet for a tandem canoe also allows it to stay on course better than a multipurpose boat. A touring model also can have lower sides, which create a shallower depth in the canoe and minimize wind resistance on lakes. However, waves can more easily enter a low-sided canoe.

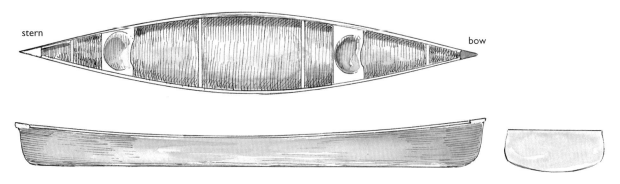

Touring canoe model. Typically 17–18 feet in length.

Multipurpose (whitewater) model

The multipurpose model suitable for whitewater canoeing is a shorter, wider boat with a blunter bow and stern. The bow is more like a finger pressing through butter! The bow and stern shown in the figure on the next page have more rounded ends or *rocker* (because the boat resembles the shape of a chair rocker), and they allow the canoe to spin around more easily with less resistance against the water. This feature is essential in whitewater to avoid obstacles and to execute playful maneuvers. However, the canoe is harder to keep tracking in a straight line. A tandem boat ranges from 15 to 16½ feet in length. Because the canoe depth is greater than in a flatwater boat, the boat sheds whitewater splash better.

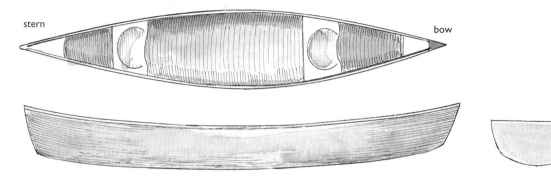

stern   bow

Whitewater canoe model. Typically 15–16½ feet in length.

TRANSPORTING THE CANOE TO WATER

I gave up trying to solo-carry a canoe years ago in order to save my back from distress. Use as many people as you need to get the canoe to the water. The following carries are described and demonstrated as two-person endeavors, but I've used four and six people to lessen the weight—canoes vary from 45 to 75 pounds. An even number of people, equally spaced on opposite sides of the canoe, creates a more balanced carry than an uneven number. Remember to bend your legs as you reach down to pick up a canoe, rather than bending from the waist, which puts excessive stress on your lower back.

Portage carry from the car rack

This overhead carry allows you to lift the canoe right off the rack with the boat already in the overturned position. Both people should face in the same direction so you are ready to walk away with the canoe. Position yourselves so that you are in front of each canoe seat. Slide the canoe across the car rack, and reach under the canoe to grab the opposite gunwale with one hand. Lift the canoe off the rack over your heads, and let the seat edge rest on the back of your neck or life jacket. Once you've arrived at the water, coordinate the lowering of the canoe. Let it roll over slowly onto your thighs (bend your legs to create a platform). Then let the canoe slide down your bent legs to rest on the ground. You can easily get two more people under the canoe for greater control when lifting it off the car and lowering it.

To place the canoe on the car rack at the end of the day, reverse the process. Slide the canoe up your legs, bending them so the canoe can rest on your thighs. On a count of three, push up with your thighs for a little extra boost and roll the canoe overhead. (See photos on page 45.)

Paula Manner, 42, a medical researcher from Seattle, Washington, has used the portage carry on wilderness trips, and she remembers an excruciatingly long portage around Dickson Canyon on the Hanbury River in the Northwest Territories. The wind prevented them from rolling the canoe up overhead, so she and her partner Michelle Dickson had to get creative in their problem solving.

"We couldn't lift the boat overhead (against the wind), and we were absolutely furious," said Paula, who is just over five feet tall. "So Michelle would lift the bow with the stern resting on the ground, and then I would back up under the stern and fight to lift it. . . . The lesson I learned was that I didn't need to be there. My body needed to be there, but I didn't need to be!"

With tall vehicles, I've taken the canoe off the car rack by pulling the end at the back of the vehicle. Two people can pull on the safety line tied to the end, until you can tilt the canoe slightly toward the ground. The first person stabilizes the canoe by standing underneath it and holding onto the gunwales. As the partner keeps pulling the boat off the rack, the first person starts "hand-walking" down the gunwales to the other end. Then the "puller" steps under the canoe to hold the gunwales, and you are both in position to lift the last end off the rack.

Door-assisted or extender-bar lift

An extender bar can be attached to your roof rack to make the lift easier. Or you can place the canoe right on the vehicle door for this one, if you are willing. Open the front door of your car or attach the extender bar to the back. One paddler slides the canoe end onto the open door or bar; the other paddler stabilizes the opposite end. Then one or both paddlers can lift the remaining end off the car and lower it to the ground. Roll the canoe over, still using the door for support. Then both paddlers stand at opposite ends to fully lower the canoe to the ground.

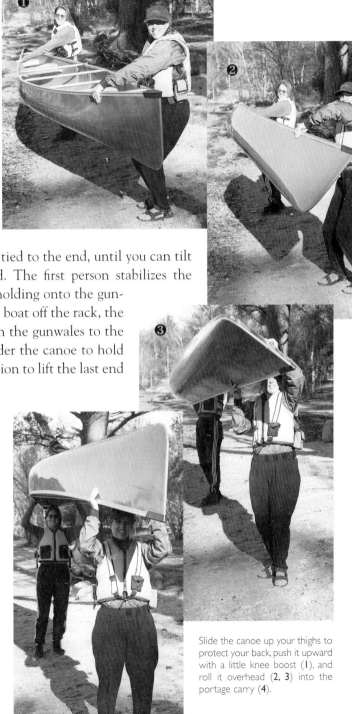

Slide the canoe up your thighs to protect your back, push it upward with a little knee boost (1), and roll it overhead (2, 3) into the portage carry (4).

Using a car door to help support the canoe can aid in lowering the canoe.

Simple upright carry

Upright carries allow you to place gear in the canoe and make only one trip to the water. The simplest carry is when two people stand at opposite ends and on opposite sides of the canoe. Both people grab onto the thwart near the deck and walk with the canoe. Don't limit yourself to two people, especially if it's a long carry. Use up to six people equally spaced on opposite sides of the canoe to get it to water, if necessary.

Canoe carts offer the same effect, where the canoe rests in an upright position and is strapped to a two-wheeled cart. The carts are easy to use at paved boat ramps and on open, sloping land. You can load up your gear and transport it to shore in just one trip. The carts get more cumbersome and unusable at steep or uneven put-ins.

A kneeling stance lowers your center of gravity and increases stability. Keep your paddle in the "ready" position.

ENTERING AND STABILIZING THE CANOE

Whether you enter the canoe from a beach or a dock, the easiest way is to enter from the side. Bear in mind that only one person should be moving around at a time in a canoe to prevent overturning it. So, as you enter the canoe, your partner should stabilize it to help you remain balanced while you move to your seat. Step carefully into the center of the canoe, just ahead of the seat, placing your hands on opposite gunwales for stability. Lower your hips as quickly as possible, because this heaviest part of your body has the single biggest impact on stability.

Whether solo or tandem canoeing, some women prefer to sit on the canoe seat while learning to paddle because their joints may be too tender for kneeling. However, if you are uncomfortable with the height, you may find that kneeling lowers your center of gravity in a reassuring way. Basketball-style kneepads are a helpful cushion as you push your knees against the sides of the canoe. Rest your buttocks against the

ROLES CANOEISTS PLAY

Now that we're ready to launch the canoe, it's time to talk about roles of each paddler in the canoe. It's easy in solo canoeing. I have to control both ends of the canoe, and the only person with whom I can argue is myself! Tandem paddling is quite different; it can be a complete joy or a wretched disaster when communication between partners starts to deteriorate. Understanding the responsibilities of each paddler can be helpful in building a good partnership.

Forget the days of the stern paddler as director or dictator of all boat action. (You may have to share this fact with a partner who didn't read the book!) The bow paddler has real responsibilities and should not be a passive spectator. It becomes especially important as you explore whitewater paddling, because the bow paddler actually initiates a lot of the action. After all, she can see the obstacles much better than the stern paddler.

The bow paddler has the following responsibilities:

- Sets the pace
- Chooses the immediate route
- Initiates turns
- In whitewater, often provides power against the current

(continued on page 48)

ROLES CANOEISTS PLAY
• • • • • • • • • • • • • • • • • •

(continued from page 47)

The stern paddler has the following responsibilities:

- Matches the pace
- Chooses the general route
- Keeps the boat on the desired general course
- In whitewater, maintains angle of canoe against the current

In whitewater canoeing, other variables become important. Who is the fastest decision-maker? Who has the best eyesight? Put that woman in the bow because she will be able to read the river features quickly and pick out the best path among them. I advocated that strategy in a *Canoe & Kayak* article on tandem communication; in an advanced clinic I gave, two women who worked at Brown University told me it had resurrected their paddling partnership! They switched positions in the canoe and found new happiness with each other and the activity.

seat for a solid three-point stance. This stance is usually used in whitewater canoeing to enhance stability in the rapids, but it is also very effective during learning and in the face of wind and waves on a lake.

The seat for a solo canoeist is just behind the midpoint of the boat. Once you are seated, you should be able to reach with your paddle toward the bow or the stern to execute your strokes. You become both the stern and bow paddler! Some women use a tandem canoe to paddle solo. They sit or rest their buttocks against the back of the bow seat, essentially paddling the canoe backward (which is fine because the boats are symmetrical). However, the easiest approach is using a shorter canoe designed specifically for the soloist. A short canoe is lighter and easier to maneuver.

So you want to stay upright at the start? While you are waiting to get started, hold your paddle and let it float almost horizontal to the water surface. This paddle position creates an outrigger that helps stabilize the canoe. It's much better than laying the paddle across the gunwales, where you have no outrigger, except one in the air! Use this "at-the-ready" position anytime you want greater stability.

Chapter 5

PADDLING STRAIGHT

If you have a touring or long, narrow canoe, it is designed to track well. You should capitalize on these characteristics by beginning your practice with the strategies described in this chapter. The "switch" style of paddling is a very rewarding way to begin, if you want to move across the water quickly with minimal frustration. The second strategy requires that you learn the J stroke, which takes more time to perfect, but you will become a more versatile paddler. If you have a short canoe that spins easily in a circle, then you are wise to begin with the turning exercises discussed in chapter 6, then return to this section to focus on paddling straight. By that time, you will have more boat and paddle "sensitivity" and will experience greater success paddling straight.

Use the technical tips here as a focus for learning, but ask other knowledgeable paddlers to watch your strokes. The best practice is perfect practice right from the beginning. Kristy

Efficient forward strokes are important in touring or racing.

Michalek, 22, a student in a Massachusetts outdoor leadership program at Greenfield Community College, said, "I needed a lot of verbal feedback. I always need somebody to tell me whether I'm doing it right, or I develop bad habits fast."

Knowing the parts of a canoe stroke is helpful:

- **catch:** the beginning of the stroke, where the blade "catches" the water fully

- **power phase:** where the paddler applies force against the paddle to move the canoe

- **exit:** the point at which the power phase ends

- **recovery:** how the blade is returned to the catch position

A paddle can be recovered to the catch in two ways: It can be (1) *feathered* above the water like the wing of a bird to reduce wind resistance, or (2) *sliced* underwater to provide stability through continuing paddle contact with the water. The feather recovery is useful when paddling large lakes; the slice recovery becomes important in the turbulence of whitewater rivers.

THE ONE-STROKE STRATEGY

The easiest way to begin paddling on flatwater is by mastering the forward stroke and using a *switch* style of paddling. Some canoeing books and articles call it the North American Touring Technique (NATT), and it works for solo and tandem paddling. You and your partner get ready to paddle on opposite sides of the canoe for good balance, executing forward strokes in unison, until just before the boat begins to veer off a straight course. Then the stern paddler calls for a switch, because she can see more easily when the canoe begins to veer. You switch paddling sides quickly and begin using forward strokes to arrest the turning until another switch is necessary. It's just as easy in a solo canoe. The soloist functions just like the stern paddler in mentally anticipating a switch in paddling sides just before the boat veers off course.

The trick is anticipating when the canoe will turn off course, because once it begins to turn, it wants to turn faster and faster! The switches need to be called earlier than you initially think. Kate McEwen, 25, a Massachusetts outdoor leadership student at Greenfield Community College, discovered that partners can coach each other effectively: "I found it hard in the stern to be coordinated at first. We definitely had to communicate about it—whether to speed up or slow down to make it work."

The action happens fast at first, but a good relationship with your partner is a key to early success. Being relaxed in your learning helps as well. Darcy Pierce, 28, also an outdoor leadership student, said, "I kept thinking: 'What do I do? Is it this? Maybe it's that! With my partner, it was trial and error to find out what worked. And it was fine."

The switch style of paddling is used by marathon racers so they can avoid steering strokes that slow the canoe, so beware! You are likely to slip into a faster and faster tempo, when you may prefer a slower style of paddling. However, the switch style is an excellent way to get moving forward quickly with minimal strokes. Your kids may love the switch style too, because they quickly gain speed, they feel like they are "going somewhere," and they may be intrigued by an approach that flirts with racing.

Leslie Johnson, 42, a nurse practitioner from Amherst, Massachusetts, has teamed up with me to compete in canoe marathons, and she loves switch paddling because of its similarity to rowing. We met on our college crew team and brought to our canoe racing that shared love of gliding fast across water.

"It's so powerful and maximizes your energy and the boat's energy. A racing boat is sleek and fast. The technique is smooth, simple, and not clumsy, because you don't waste any time steering," she said. "You're flying along the river, and you can actually pick up the pace when you need to. You really feel like you are together with the water when you have it right."

To refine your switch paddling, use these focuses:

- synchronized strokes to consistently propel the canoe forward

- an early switch of paddling sides (before the canoe veers too far off course)

- efficient forward strokes that provide forward power rather than turning action

An efficient forward stroke

Today's emphasis on "torso" paddling helps women paddle more strongly and encounter less fatigue. Rather than using just the weaker arm muscles, the best stroke relies on the larger, stronger muscles of the torso to power the canoe. You'll feel your abdominal and back muscles get into the act so that canoeing becomes more of a "total body" experience! Consequently, you can paddle farther with less effort.

Some women still try to muscle their way through the forward stroke at first, using their arms too much. But fatigue can actually be a benefit because it can serve as a wake-up call about your technique. Jackie Waite, an outdoor leadership student from Hatfield, Massachusetts, said, "I found when I was tired, it was a lot easier to use my back than my arms to do the forward stroke." Jackie discovered that when your strength no longer allows you to compensate, you have to use good technique.

Catch position for the forward stroke.

TIPS FOR FORWARD STROKES

- Tight, white knuckles mean tension in your grip. Wiggle your fingers to relax.
- Bending your arms weakens your brace against the paddle. Keep the elbows relatively straight through the power and recovery phases.
- If your grip hand drifts inside the boat in front of your chest, it puts a sweeping action on the stroke that sends you off course. Push your top hand out over the water.
- Excessive bending at the waist makes the canoe bob or "porpoise" through the water, and it tires your lower back. Bend forward slightly at the catch to get a better reach (about 10 degrees from straight upright). Remember that the real power comes from the torso untwisting.

Follow these six steps to increase efficiency in your forward stroke:

- Swivel or rotate your torso to slip the blade into the water at the catch. Your shoulders and chest should feel coiled around a central axis (i.e., your spine). The shoulder closest to the paddle is extended forward as far as you can comfortably twist and reach (1).

- Keep both hands over the water so the paddle shaft is vertical to the water surface when looking from the front.

- Uncoil your torso to propel the paddle through the water in an imaginary line parallel to the canoe's centerline. Keep your arms comfortably straight so your torso engages well (2).

Swivel your torso to plant the paddle at the catch (1), and rotate your torso to apply force against the paddle (2). Slide the paddle sideways out of the water (3) and feather it back to the catch (4).

- Think of the paddle as a brace against the water and thrust your hips forward past the blade. Because a woman's mass is mostly in the hips, you can really feel your hips propel the boat forward.

- Let your paddle slide sideways out of the water when the blade passes your hip (3).

- Return your paddle to the catch position by feathering or flattening it to the water surface (4).

Remember these basic principles as you continue to learn to paddle. They can be applied to all canoeing and kayaking strokes to improve your efficiency.

PADDLING FORWARD WITH THE J STROKE

Learning additional strokes can make you a more precise paddler and prepare you for longer flat-water tours and a transition to current. Then you can combine them in various ways to create the maneuvers that make paddling a graceful and exciting endeavor.

The *J stroke* is useful to move any canoe forward on a straight course, but it has been dusted off and updated since you learned it at summer camp. Using it is more skillful than switch paddling and harder to learn, but it's well worth the effort to improve your boat-handling skills. Besides, it makes you feel like a pro in the back of the canoe! The stern paddler uses the stroke in combination with forward strokes; the trick is to execute both, as needed, while staying synchronized with your bow partner's forward strokes.

The J stroke begins just like the forward stroke, with some important changes.

1. At the catch, position the blade under the hull with your grip (top) hand out over the water (see upper left photo).

2. Uncoil your torso, keeping the blade under the hull through the beginning of the stroke (see upper left photo).

3. Slide the paddle shaft along the boat to position it against the gunwale for good leverage.

4. As the blade passes your knee, change the angle of the blade by rotating your grip hand away from your body and pointing your thumb forward. Keep a loose grip with your shaft (lower) hand so the paddle can swivel to the correct position.

Position the blade under the canoe to begin the J stroke (1). Then roll your "grip" thumbs down toward the water for the proper blade angle (2, 3). To reduce wind resistance during the recovery, orient the blade until the leading edge is perpendicular to the wind direction (4).

5.   Slide the blade into position slightly behind your hip in a touring canoe.

6.   Press the paddle grip into the canoe slightly, which forces the blade outward in a "J" path. The paddle shaft against the gunwale provides good leverage to do this.

7.   The blade stays less than a foot from the canoe at the end of the stroke (any farther and it inhibits forward momentum).

8.   Let the blade slide forward with no resistance from the water until it rises to the surface.

9.   Return the paddle to the catch position.

With today's stronger canoes and paddles, levering the J stroke off the boat works great for women. The canoe creates much stronger leverage than you could with your muscles; the equipment takes the stress, not your joints.

Mary Grover, 37, a school administrator from Charlemont, Massachusetts, has paddled the difficult stretches of the upper Deerfield River for many years, but she recently refined her strokes in a canoe instructor workshop. "The J stroke has been the most difficult for me. Then I figured out that I was turning my upper hand the wrong way." She realized her top thumb needed to be turned *away* from her body to use the powerface of the blade throughout the entire stroke, and she also swiveled the blade into position *early*, just past the catch position. Then she added the final touch: "For it to be a powerful stroke for me, I need a levering action off the boat—a quick flick. That's really powerful for me."

Left: For a quicker J stroke, keep your grip hand high and J near your hip. Then slice the paddle forward to begin the recovery. **Right:** Let the paddle lift naturally from the water and reorient it to begin another stroke.

TIPS FOR J STROKES

- Keep your grip hand out over the water. This keeps the blade firmly under the canoe, where it can use the roiled water effectively to carve the J and turn the stern end.

- Sink the blade deep enough in the water during the J phase so it actually pushes against the water and moves your stern strongly away from the blade.

- Make sure the powerface of the blade is pushing sideways against the water throughout the entire stroke. (If you switch to the backface during the J phase, then you're doing a turning stroke called a *pry*. The pry works quite well to turn the stern end, but it does slow the boat more than the J.) See chapter 6 for a look at the pry.

- Hold the shaft of the paddle against the canoe with your hand just above or below the gunwale so you don't pinch your fingers. The exact hand position will vary depending on your torso and arm length.

- As you carve the J, check the wrist of your shaft hand. It should be straight in alignment with your forearm. If your wrist is bent, you are putting enormous stress on the joint. Instead, let the shaft rotate within your grasp to angle the blade.

The stern paddler's challenge is matching the pace of her partner, which means keeping all strokes synchronized to develop consistent forward power. The J may take a little longer to execute at the beginning, so the stern paddler may need to hurry through the forward-stroke phase at the outset or quicken her recovery of the blade back to the catch.

SOLO CANOE STRATEGIES

You can use the same two options in a solo canoe: Adopt the switch style in a flatwater canoe that tracks well and learn the J stroke for a boat that turns more quickly. Because you are sitting in the middle of the canoe, your strokes can send the boat off course more quickly. You need to develop a quicker sensitivity to this tendency, executing your strokes in a quicker fashion. Expect to zigzag at the start, as you develop a sense of how to keep the boat on course. In some canoes, the gunwales bulge outward at the midpoint, just where you want to execute the J stroke, so it's extremely important to make sure the blade comes under the boat as you carve the J through the water. Another trick is leaning the canoe slightly toward your paddle, which drops the gunwale and gets it out of your way.

However, a nifty stroke called the *cross forward* can be very useful in keeping the canoe on course. The cross forward is similar to the forward stroke, except you perform it on the other side of the canoe to prevent the boat from turning. You don't change your original grip on the paddle; simply lift the paddle across the canoe and place it in the water.

Follow these steps to learn a cross forward (see photo next page).

1. Lift the paddle from your original canoeing side and lean forward about 50 degrees from an upright position to place it in the water on the opposite side.

2. Your arms are comfortably extended forward, and the paddle is vertical to the water surface at the catch.

3. Place the paddle in the water next to the canoe without touching it.

4. Lift your torso to apply power to the paddle and scoot your hips past the paddle.

5. Keep the paddle vertical to the water surface; think of it as a pole that stays upright.

6. When the paddle approaches your knee, prepare to change the blade angle to return it to the catch position.

7. Point your top thumb forward (away from you) to angle the blade parallel to the canoe.

8. Slice the paddle underwater back to the catch; let it rise to the surface if water pushes it around.

9. To begin another stroke, swivel the blade until it is perpendicular to the centerline again.

Lean forward to get into the catch position for the **cross-forward stroke**.

Develop a quick back-and-forth rhythm with the blade through a lowering and raising of the upper body to perform a number of cross-forward strokes. Again, your torso is the machine here, and women find the stroke to be a powerful one in arresting any veering. In fact, you may find that you "overcorrect" and have to tone down the cross-forward. It's one of my favorite strokes because the upper-body lift makes it extremely effective.

Now put these strokes together to paddle in a straight line. If you want to test your control, choose a point on shore and paddle toward it. Use a combination of forward and cross-forward strokes to keep the canoe on course. The trick is anticipating *when* the canoe will veer off course, not *if*! It happens after only a few strokes in a multipurpose canoe; add several more strokes in a flatwater canoe.

Chapter 6

If you use a multipurpose canoe having ends that are more rockered (curved) than those of flat-water canoes, then the boat wants to spin off course more readily than a sleeker flatwater model. With a multipurpose boat, you are wise to begin your practice by capitalizing on what it does best. Why fight the physical forces?

First I address basic strokes that help you spin the canoe in place. Then I suggest how to modify the basic strokes so you can turn while moving across the water. Here, the water hits the canoe in different ways and demands some subtle adjustments of the original strokes. Your practice should begin on flatwater, but both of these moves are essential to whitewater canoeing later.

Two terms may be useful, especially if you are trying to communicate with a partner about which way to turn. In an *onside* turn, the canoe turns toward the designated paddling side of the bow (or solo) paddler. In an *offside* turn, the canoe turns away from the designated paddling side of the bow (or solo) paddler. These more descriptive terms are better than "left" and "right" calls, which often confuse people.

THE ONSIDE SPIN WITH A DRAW STROKE

This stroke may seem like an old friend because it has been taught in camp canoeing programs since the turn of the century. The *draw* moves your end of a tandem canoe toward the blade, and

TIPS FOR DRAW STROKES
• • • • • • • • • • • • • • • • • •

- Keep your top hand fairly stationary throughout the draw stroke. Let the paddle hang from your hand like the pendulum on a clock. If your top hand comes inside the gunwale, you are working too hard with bent arms.

- Make your bottom hand do most of the work. It stabilizes the paddle, particularly during the underwater recovery.

- Make sure partners paddle in unison. Then you'll feel bolder about reaching well away from the canoe at the catch for a big bite of water.

it can be used simultaneously by bow and stern paddlers to spin the boat. Your goal is to execute the strokes simultaneously so the boat spins smoothly rather than wobbles from side to side through the turn.

Follow these steps in performing the draw stroke:

1. Place the paddle in the water opposite your hip and as far from the canoe as you can comfortably reach. Both arms, especially the top arm, extend fully for good reach (bottom left).

2. Rotate your torso until your shoulders face the blade; think of it as always facing your work.

3. Keep your top hand over the water during the stroke; the paddle stays upright or vertical to the water surface as a result.

4. Move your hips toward the blade; stop before the blade hits the canoe.

5. Swivel your top hand by rotating your thumb away from your body. The blade now will be perpendicular to the centerline but still buried in the water (bottom right).

Above: Keep the paddle vertical for the catch position for the draw.
Right: The draw recovery is an underwater slice.

6. Slice the blade underwater back to the catch position.

7. Swivel your top hand (your thumb points backward) until the blade is parallel to the centerline and ready for the next stroke.

ONSIDE U-TURN WHILE UNDERWAY

Now that you've practiced a tighter spin in place, you can modify the maneuver as you move across the water. Perhaps you want to swing right into position next to a dock and impress an audience on shore with your boat control! You also can take this maneuver to the river and use it to turn in behind a rock.

Plant the paddle like a post for the **Duffek stroke** in the bow.

You can easily modify the basic draw stroke into a *Duffek* stroke, which gives great stability and turning power when underway. In the bow or solo position, place the paddle in the water in a slightly different catch position than the draw stroke. Rather than opposite your hip, slide the paddle forward and inward about 6 inches. Most importantly, angle the powerface of the blade toward the oncoming water so the blade can be braced against and "catch" this water. If you use the original blade angle for the draw (parallel to the centerline), the blade will simply slice through the oncoming water without catching it. Think of planting the paddle like you would grab a post and swing around it (just like the boat will swing around your planted paddle).

However, once you feel the water pressure begin to fade under your blade, you have two choices. If you still need to turn the canoe, keep doing more draws toward the bow. If you have completed the turn, change to forward strokes to continue moving forward or to stay behind the rock in the river. Thinking too long and doing nothing? Well, you might find yourself tipping over the canoe if the water isn't bracing against the paddle!

So far, the action seems to be in the bow. You're right! The turn happens mostly on the strength of the bow paddler's stroke. However, the stern paddler does play a role here. In the stern, you'll feel the oncoming water begin to push your draw stroke backward if you try to use that stroke. Don't fight the water! Abandon the draw stroke for a *forward sweep*, which is more efficient.

The forward sweep

A stern paddler can use a forward sweep very effectively in turning the canoe while moving because the stroke offers the dual functions of momentum and turning in one easy package. The forward sweep has been a summer-camp favorite for 100 years, but it has a new look! Now it is also a stroke driven by your torso rather than just your arms.

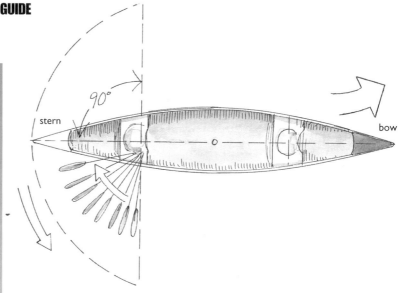

A **forward sweep** in the stern.

TIPS FOR FORWARD SWEEP STROKES

• • • • • • • • • • • • • • • • • •

- If the boat barely moves or your arms get tired, you probably aren't using your torso.
- Check your grip hand. If it's inside the gunwale and high around your chest, the paddle is too near the pivot point. You are not reaching away from the canoe enough during the stroke.

It's useful to think of the action happening in a 90 degree quadrant formed by your hip and the centerline of the canoe behind your body. The sweep is an arcing stroke that occurs within this quadrant, and it functions best when it is executed as far away from the canoe's pivot point as possible. The pivot point is often the canoe's midpoint, where the boat rests most deeply in the water and encounters the greatest resistance. As a result, a sweep is most effective near the rounded ends of the canoe, where water resistance against the boat is lessened.

Above: Extend the paddle horizontally to the water surface opposite your hip. **Right and far right:** Let your eyes follow the blade to engage the torso when sweeping.

Follow these steps to perform the forward sweep stroke:

1. Plant the paddle shaft horizontally to the water surface opposite your hip.

2. Extend your shaft arm fully and comfortably to reach away from the canoe and its pivot point.

3. Rotate your torso around, trying to get your shoulders parallel with the centerline. Let your eyes and shoulders follow the paddle. This makes your larger trunk muscles apply force against the paddle.

4. Keep your shaft arm straight early in the stroke—it forces your trunk to be active. Your arm may bend slightly as the paddle exits the water.

5. Before the paddle strikes the canoe, recover the blade by feathering it back to the catch position. The powerface should face the sky on the recovery.

THE OFFSIDE SPIN

Now you want to spin the canoe the other way. Some canoeists will simply switch paddling sides and repeat the previous maneuvers. It's the simplest approach! However, if your goal is whitewater canoeing, where switching sides can cost you crucial time and stability, then take the time to learn several new strokes using your original clasp on the paddle. The bow paddler gets to experiment with a "cross" stroke called a *cross draw*, and the stern canoeist learns a pry. A cross stroke occurs when a bow paddler moves her paddle from the original paddling side to the opposite side of the canoe—without changing her original grip on the paddle.

The cross draw

The cross draw has the opposite effect of a draw stroke: it moves the bow of the canoe the other way. You reach across the bow

TIPS FOR CROSS DRAW STROKES
. . . .

- Watch your shaft arm. If it bends, you are using your arms to power the stroke. Keeping your shaft arm straight forces your torso to do the work.

- Keep your torso upright so it can wind and unwind nicely through the stroke. If you lean forward, you'll compromise your torso's ability to power the stroke and your ability to lean the canoe.

- Keep your grip hand low. It keeps the paddle more horizontal, which means the blade stays farther from the pivot point and can turn the boat more easily.

Point your grip thumb toward the sky with the **cross draw**.

> "I like the cross draw. It came really naturally. I felt like I could do it in a strong manner and be efficient."
>
> —Kate McEwen

as in the photo above, opposite your original paddling side, and use the cross draw to pull the canoe toward the blade. The cross draw is a handy bow stroke that works well for women because it relies on the coiling of your torso. The stroke requires some flexibility in your upper body, but even a small reach across the bow will pay big dividends. The action twists your torso in a new direction in a tight coil, so the uncoiling is especially forceful.

Kate McEwen, an outdoor leadership program student, said, "I like the cross draw. It came really naturally. I felt like I could do it in a strong manner and be efficient."

Follow these steps in practicing the cross draw:

1.   Lift the paddle across the bow and rotate your torso as far as your flexibility allows. Your shoulders face away from the canoe. (See photo this page.)

2.   Move the paddle into a position more horizontal to the water surface, with the thumb of your grip hand pointing toward the sky. (See photo this page.)

3.   The powerface of the blade faces the canoe.

4.   Your shaft arm extends fully at the catch and stays extended throughout the stroke. Your grip hand remains low—between your hip and chest.

5.   Swivel your torso until your shoulders are perpendicular to the centerline, which will bring the bow to the blade.

6.   Lift the blade from the water before the canoe strikes it, and recover the blade to the catch position.

The stern pry

The stern paddler needs to spin her end of the canoe as well, and a *pry stroke* works well to quickly push the stern away from the stroke. The pry uses the canoe as leverage, so this mechanical advantage makes it a strong stroke. Again, you save your joints and muscles from any extra work. When partners do the cross draw and stern pry at the same time, the canoe spins quickly in place.

Follow these steps to perform the pry stroke in the stern:

1.   Move the paddle into position by aligning it with the gunwale, horizontal to the water.

2.   Rotate your shoulders around so they face the paddle and the gunwale. (It's easier to control the paddle this way.)

• •

"**T**he pry was hard at first. I felt like my hand wasn't big enough to hold the paddle. Then I learned you don't have to hold it. You can rest your shaft hand on the gunwale."

—Kate McEwen

• •

TIPS FOR PRY STROKES
• • • • • • • • • • • • • • • • • •

- A long pull on the paddle will move it too far from the canoe and destroy your oarlock, or grip on the oars, especially if you have small hands. Keep the stroke short.

- Make sure you create the lever behind your body, nearer the rockered ends of the canoe, where resistance against the water is lessened.

The **stern pry**.

3.   Let the thumb of your shaft hand anchor the shaft to the gunwale. If you have small hands, use the heel of your hand on top of the gunwale to create a fulcrum (fixed point).

4.   Create this "oarlock" or leverage point just behind your rear end, so the blade is near the stern of the canoe.

5.   Slide the paddle shaft through the oarlock so the entire blade rests in the water near the stern.

6.   The powerface faces away from the canoe; the backface is against the canoe.

7.   Pull in with your grip hand about 6 inches to force the blade away from the canoe.

8.   Drop your grip hand near the gunwale so the blade lifts free of the water and can be returned to the catch position.

I think of the pry as an "eggbeater" stroke—short and quick to "froth" the water. Lots of little prys will turn the canoe quickly by pushing the stern away from your paddle. You can't really paddle in unison with your partner during an offside spin. The cross draw is a longer stroke than the pry. Think of equalizing your power rather than stroke rates; the strokes use different mechanisms for turning.

Kate McEwen said, "The pry was hard at first. I felt like my hand wasn't big enough to hold the paddle. Then I learned you don't have to hold it. You can rest your shaft hand on the gunwale."

OFFSIDE U-TURN WHILE UNDERWAY

Once you've practiced a quick offside spin in place, it's time to experiment with an offside U-turn while moving. Perhaps you want to execute a really flashy move approaching the boat dock or turning in behind a rock in the river. The offside U-turn is guaranteed to please family and friends, and you'll find it a fun move! Some simple modifications of the previous strokes are helpful.

Let's modify the bow paddler's cross draw into a *cross Duffek*. At the catch shown in the illustration on the following page, the orientation of the paddle shaft changes to a more vertical position relative to the water surface to give you more stability. As a result, the blade will move closer to your body. To help create this solid brace against the water, let both arms extend as fully as possible when the paddle is in the catch position.

After you gain momentum with forward strokes, plant the paddle in the cross Duffek position and hold the paddle still. Your paddle creates a fixed point or anchor around which the canoe will turn. When the bow swings around toward the paddle, you'll feel the water pressure

Hold a **cross Duffek** (bow) stationary as a point around which the canoe will turn (**1**). The reverse sweep in the stern also helps to create the **tandem offside turn** (**2, 3**). The bow turns naturally toward the cross Duffek as the sweep ends (**4**).

begin to fade under the blade. Then you must decide whether to do a cross draw to continue turning or a forward stroke to move the canoe into position behind the rock. You also can borrow a stroke from solo canoeists and use a cross forward (see page 57) after the cross Duffek to complete the move.

What does the stern paddler do? She can use the pry for a quick turn, or try a reverse sweep for a longer, slower turn.

The reverse sweep

A stern paddler can use a *reverse sweep* very smoothly in an offside U-turn to move the stern away from the paddle. The stroke happens in a 90-degree quadrant behind your body, with an angle formed by your hip and the centerline of the canoe. The path of the sweep creates an arc within this quadrant; it is particularly effective near the rounded end of the stern, where resistance against the water is lessened.

Follow these steps to perform the reverse sweep stroke:

1. Rotate your torso around, trying to get your shoulders parallel with the center-line, to get the paddle into position next to the canoe.

2. Keep your grip hand low so the shaft is more horizontal to the water surface, which locates the blade closer to the stern end.

TIPS FOR REVERSE SWEEP STROKES

- Keep your hands over the water or near the gunwale when performing the stroke. If your grip hand creeps inside the boat in front of your body, the blade will end up closer to the canoe's pivot point, where water resistance is greater.

- Check the catch position. The paddle should enter the water near the canoe so you don't miss the early turning force here.

"If you want more stability from the reverse sweep, you can flatten the blade against the water surface as you sweep it."

3. The backface of the blade is ready to push against the water. Your grip thumb points up toward the sky.

4. Bend your arms slightly at the catch position, and begin pushing the canoe away from the blade with a torso swivel. (I've always felt stronger with slightly bent arms when I'm pushing away from my body because locking my arms in a bent position and holding them close to my body seems to drive the stroke.)

5. Let your shaft arm straighten to finish the stroke. It keeps the paddle farther away from the pivot point.

6. Stop the stroke when the blade is opposite your hip. Recover the blade to the catch position with the powerface facing the sky on the recovery.

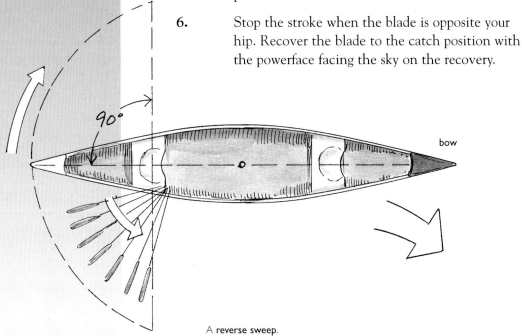

A reverse sweep.

If you want more stability from the reverse sweep, you can flatten the blade against the water surface as you sweep it. Turn the knuckles of your hand down toward the water, which presses the blade's backface against the water. It moves you into a *low brace* position, where the paddle functions like an outrigger for balance. Remember to elevate the blade's leading edge as you sweep so the paddle keeps rising to the water surface.

TURNING A SOLO CANOE

You can mix and match the previous strokes to turn a solo canoe. Choose any of them! Think of it this way: a solo paddler has two roles that she can adopt. If she functions like a bow paddler, she can use the Duffek to turn the canoe toward her paddle (onside turn) or the cross Duffek (offside turn) to move the canoe the other way. The Duffeks often allow for snappier turns because the paddle provides a solid pivot point around which the canoe will spin. If the solo paddler functions like a stern paddler, she can use a reverse sweep (onside turn) or a forward sweep (offside turn) for a slower, more flowing turn.

You also can use a combination of those strokes to adjust the precision of the turn, particularly in whitewater situations. For example, you can start an onside turn with a reverse sweep to begin to turn the canoe behind a rock and slow it down slightly. Then convert the stroke to a Duffek to finish the turn, which means you must flip the blade from its backface (on the sweep) to the powerface (on the Duffek). It's a nifty move that feels incredibly graceful.

LEANING A CANOE

The shape of a canoe can affect a turn tremendously. Don't get discouraged if a sleeker canoe is hard to turn. Just plan enough distance for a longer, slower turn before you reach the dock! Remember that a curved boat is likely to turn faster and more easily because the ends slide more easily in the water. You can build on that same principle and experience an easier turn by adding boat lean to your moves.

If you lean a canoe on its side, you tend to lift the ends out of the water and reduce the surface resistance against the water. You create a more rockered canoe by leaning it, which is easier to do from a lower, kneeling stance. Shifting your weight onto one knee will tilt the canoe toward that side and make it easier to turn the canoe that way—faster, too! Tandem paddlers need to shift their weight in unison so the boat doesn't bobble or flip. It's a strategy that makes a turn very rewarding.

Now, this doesn't mean that you lean your bodies excessively outside the canoe, unless you desire that artistic effect in freestyle canoeing. Think of it as *boat* lean, not *body* lean. Your trunk stays relatively upright in the canoe, right above the knee over which you are balanced. You'll feel a stretch in your side over the "balancing knee" and a scrunch in the other side where your hip has lifted this gunwale. Your body forms a J, as shown in the illustration on page 73. This knee-and-hip action moves the canoe under you and tilts it on its side. Keeping your trunk centered not only provides stability, it also allows you to switch to different maneuvers quickly and subtly.

The J lean is used in river- and sea-kayaking, and women use it very successfully. We tend to carry a lot of our mass in the big pelvic bones, which keeps our center of gravity fairly low. You'll be amazed at how stable it feels; the payoff in quicker, less "muscular" turns is huge.

Chapter 7

YOUR RESCUE RESPONSIBILITIES

Cathy Piffath practicing throwing a rescue bag.

Developing rescue skills is an integral part of learning to canoe. You have a responsibility to take care of yourself when paddling, and it's important that your rescue skills be as well developed as your canoeing ability. Today, too many people flock to paddlesports without knowing how to safely recover from a capsize. To be properly prepared, every canoeist must also wear or carry essential rescue gear (discussed in chapter 8). It's an important mindset that prepares you for the possibility that no one will arrive to assist you. Your confidence with self-rescue is ultimately what allows you to embrace more challenging canoeing. An important question to ask yourself when contemplating whether to run a rapid is whether you are willing to swim it. If you accept the possibility of swimming, then you are prepared for anything the rapid can deliver!

• •

"I still have a healthy respect for rapids and rough water. But I don't fear them, because I believe my judgment and skills give me the insight and confidence to handle various conditions."

—Becky Mason

• •

Often, women envision big waves on lakes or dancing whitewater as the cause of a capsize, but it's usually much simpler and more benign. A capsize can happen right at shore when the dog jumps out of the canoe and overturns it! Poor swimmers can be very nervous about capsizing, but remember this fact: A good life jacket will float your head high above the water, even if you are a big person. I recommend that you practice capsizing on your own terms because it's the key to becoming a more relaxed canoeist. Choose a warm day or a heated pool with a group of friends and practice swimming in a life jacket, as well as rescuing the canoe. It will make you feel much better about your ability to handle the situation, and your canoe tours will become less tension-filled and more enjoyable.

The safest way to canoe is in the company of other paddlers because they can help rescue you. You and your family can have a wonderful time practicing the rescues; kids like to overturn canoes, especially on a hot day. Just be aware that quieter people may be experiencing a little apprehension at first; let them decide when and where to capsize the canoe—near shore may be the best place to begin.

Becky Mason, 34, of Chelsea, Quebec, also recommends that people practice self-rescue skills first in calm, warm water and then in rougher conditions, until the response becomes second nature. "I find that time and time again, people are embarrassed about the thought that they might tip their canoe. I do not have that problem in the least because my dad taught us that tipping and rescuing was just another important skill to be learned and done well."

Practicing rescues in current is as important as it is in flatwater because it's easier if your first river swims are deliberate and controlled. Becky remembers her first strong memory of canoeing, at six years old, was swimming the Blue Chute on the French River: "We tipped on purpose because my Dad wanted to get a realistic wipeout scene to include in his film *Song of the Paddle*. I remember smashing through those waves with my paddle and then bobbing up to the surface in my life jacket, thinking this rapid running was loads of fun! This particular incident was a positive experience because my Dad prepared us well by telling us what would happen when we tipped in the rapid. I still have a healthy respect for rapids and rough water. But I don't fear them, because I believe my judgment and skills give me the insight and confidence to handle various situations."

In this chapter, you'll learn the fundamentals of self- and group-rescue. No two rescue scenes are alike, so you'll have to judge each situation and determine which type of rescue is appropriate at the moment. The appropriate safety gear that you need on paddling trips is addressed in chapter 8, "Getting Equipped."

CAPSIZE PREVENTION

Capsizing is preventable, but certainly not by grabbing the gunwales. That's the last thing you want to do, because you'll pull the canoe right over with you as you roll over. Instead, use your paddle as an outrigger to stabilize the boat. New canoeists like the "resting position" introduced in chapter 4, where they let the paddle float gently in the water when they aren't performing a stroke. This outrigger can be converted quickly to two different kinds of bracing strokes that keep the canoe upright.

The high brace

When the canoe starts to tip *away* from your paddle, you can use the *high brace* to prevent it from rolling farther. Quickly change the paddle from the resting position to the upright orientation where the paddle shaft is vertical to the water surface. It's the starting position for the draw stroke described in chapter 6, where the fully immersed blade keeps good contact with the water. The paddle sticks in the water like glue and prevents the canoe from overturning farther.

Follow these steps to perform a high brace:

1. From the resting position, quickly punch your grip hand away from the canoe until the paddle is vertical to the water surface.

A high brace.

**TIPS FOR
HIGH BRACES**
• • • • • • • • • • • • • • • • •

- React quickly!
- Dig the blade deeply into the water.
- Never rest your paddle across the gunwales in a rapid, because you can't get to a high brace fast enough, should it be necessary.

TIPS FOR
LOW BRACES

• • • • • • • • • • • • • • • •

- Check your knuckles to ensure that they are facing downward; get them wet to make sure the paddle is low enough to the water!

- Let the foot farthest from your paddle hook under the canoe seat to increase your body's connection with the canoe.

2.   Keep the blade immersed deeply in the water.

3.   Push downward on your knee or hip closest to the paddle to arrest the canoe roll.

If the canoe is tipping aggressively away from the paddle, convert the stroke to an active draw toward your hip so the blade remains stuck in the water.

At a more advanced level, you can also slice the paddle right under the canoe until the shaft rests against the boat. The slice involves reorienting the blade face from parallel to the boat to perpendicular to it. The blade cuts throught the water with minimal resistance until it reaches the canoe. Then quickly reorient the blade to a parallel position and pull the paddle grip inward and down—forcefully dropping the gunwale and in essence prying against the canoe to right it.

The low brace

What happens when the canoe tips *toward* the side where you are paddling? A high brace will dive straight to the lake bottom, taking you with it. Instead, a *low brace* is helpful when the canoe wants to roll you toward your paddle. The low brace shown here

A low brace.

is an outrigger that can stabilize a canoe in this situation. It is performed best from a kneeling position with a lowered center of gravity. (Many canoeists move to their knees when paddling in wind and waves because a sitting position raises the center of gravity and makes the canoe tippier.)

Kneel in the canoe with your paddle in the resting or at-the-ready position, and follow these steps to perform a low brace:

> "**C**apsizing is preventable, but certainly not by grabbing the gunwales. That's the last thing you want to do, because you'll pull the canoe right over with you as you roll over."

1. Without changing your grip on the paddle, roll the blade over so the backface presses against the water.

2. Face your grip-hand knuckles down toward the water to roll the paddle over.

3. Keep the paddle shaft perpendicular to the centerline for the strongest brace.

4. Extend the paddle away from the canoe so your grip hand is near or in the water, which keeps the blade near the water surface.

5. Press down on the knee closest to the paddle to move the gunwale out of the way and lean the canoe to simulate the capsize.

6. Press the blade against the water and quickly use this pressure as a platform from which to push yourself and the canoe upright.

7. Push down on the knee and hip farthest from the paddle to bring the canoe back to a neutral position.

8. Slide the paddle shaft back toward the canoe as you remove the lean to level the canoe, and return the paddle to the resting position.

ACTIVE SELF-RESCUE IN FLATWATER

A capsize is often a surprise, so even the best braces may occur too late to save the canoe from rolling over. What happens when a canoeist becomes a swimmer? Even a group-rescue is based on the capsized paddler's ability to help with the rescue. It's important to remember that swimming is an inherent part of canoeing that many have experienced. Rachelle Bourque, 56, a wildlife artist from Roque Bluffs, Maine, remembers a big-river moment that didn't stop her from becoming a canoe guide: "I capsized and went down a Class IV drop on the Rio Grande in Texas. I thought my life was through, but I just got a bruised wrist and lost my hat."

What enables you to recover from a capsize on flatwater? Remember these priorities:

- **People.** Assess the safety of your own location; check whether your partner and passengers are okay.

- **Canoe.** Stay near the canoe, holding onto the safety lines, unless it is unsafe to do so.

- **Gear.** Clasp your paddle if you can, but allow your waterproofed gear to bob in the water.

If you are canoeing alone, you will have to swim the canoe to shore to empty it out. This reality is a good reason for choosing a conservative route near shore when traveling alone on lakes. Becky Mason believes that solo novices should develop a good, healthy respect for the land and water because conditions can change rapidly from flat calm to unruly wind storms. "This and other situations won't be a problem if you think about and put into practice a rule I teach to my Classic Solo students. 'You should never paddle farther from shore than you can swim or self-rescue.'" She recommends a 15-foot rule from shore since most people can swim that far in icy spring or autumn water.

The quickest self-rescue is to swim directly to a nearby shore. Swim with your boat if the weather allows it. But if you risk becoming too cold, swim only with your bag of spare clothing so that you can change quickly on shore. The canoe can be retrieved later.

Or paddle your swamped canoe to shore. When you roll the canoe upright, it remains swamped and wobbly in the water. Climb into the submerged craft, and paddle this wallowing submarine to shore!

Forget other recommended procedures in old paddling books, such as swimming under the overturned boat, executing a Capistrano flip where you lift the canoe above the water surface, draining it of water, and rolling it upright. It doesn't work unless you have an aluminum canoe with flotation chambers in each end and a muscle-bound partner. Nor do "shakeouts" work, where you push a swamped but upright canoe rapidly forward to drain out water, then lift the canoe end sharply to prevent water from flowing back in. It takes more brute strength than most people have. This action still leaves the canoe really full of water and requires lots (hours) of bailing! The moral here is don't paddle alone unless you are willing to get yourself to shore by paddling a swamped canoe or swimming it in.

• •

"I capsized and went down a Class IV drop on the Rio Grande in Texas. I thought my life was through, but I just got a bruised wrist and lost my hat."

—Rachelle Bourque, age 54

• •

ASSISTING WITH A FLATWATER RESCUE

The quickest rescues are those in which other canoeists can come to your assistance. With just a little practice, novices can become effective rescuers who are able to get swimmers back into their boat in under two minutes. It's an essential skill if you plan to paddle in seasons or locations where the water is cold.

The rescuers have specific responsibilities as a rescue operation is unfolding. While the swimming canoeists are actively beginning their self-rescue, you must:

1.   Yell "Canoe!" to alert other paddlers about the capsize.

2.   Stop and assess the overall scene.

3.   Check to ensure that the swimmers are okay.

4.   Develop a rescue plan that is communicated to other paddlers, including the swimmers.

5.   Stand by and do nothing if other boats are assisting with the rescue.

A rescuer has a responsibility to avoid complicating the situation further if other canoes are involved in the rescue. Once you have checked that the swimmers and canoe are being rescued, you can begin to collect accessory gear. Don't do anything to jeopardize your own safety because you will complicate the unfolding rescue if you also tip over.

Stay calm and respond without accelerating the frenzy that can develop at a rescue scene. Lucille Rossignol, 26, an outdoor leadership program student, said after her first practice, "The rescues were a little frantic. I wished we had slowed down." That's good advice because the goal is to execute rescues smoothly without inflicting further injury.

The simplest assisted rescue is *towing* the capsized craft to a nearby shore. Canoeists in the closest boat can paddle near the swimmers and let the swimmers hold onto the stern safety line of the rescue craft. Meanwhile, the swimmers also are holding onto the safety line attached to the swamped canoe. The rescuers must paddle hard directly to shore. Encourage the swimmers to kick hard to help move the canoe forward; a boat filled with water is extremely heavy.

The T rescue

An easy procedure on flatwater is a *catamaran* or *T rescue*, which allows you to empty the swamped canoe and rescue the swimmers into it. It's handy to know for a capsize far from shore. The name comes from the formation created when the rescue canoes position them-selves perpendicular to the capsized craft. The best T rescue involves two rescue canoes side by side in a catamaran; the boats are more stable when the rescuers lift the swamped canoe from the water. One canoe can perform a T rescue, but it takes very good balance from the rescuers.

Two rescue canoes form a T with the swamped boat.

Follow these steps to execute a T rescue:

1. The closest canoeists paddle toward one end of the capsized canoe and position their boat so that it forms a "T" perpendicular to the swamped craft.

2. The swimmers can hold onto the rescue canoe or they can swim to opposite ends of the capsized canoe to help with the rescue.

3. The second rescue boat paddles into position parallel to the first rescue canoe. These new rescuers hold together the gunwales of the two canoes to create a stable catamaran formation.

4. The primary rescuers lift one end of the overturned canoe from the water and rest it on their gunwale.

5. The swimmers can push down and push up on their ends of the swamped canoe to help the rescuers break the suction.

6. The primary rescuers slide the canoe across the catamaran, emptying out the water.

7. The swimmers can help push the canoe across the gunwales, and they'll end up at the catamaran.

8. Once the overturned canoe is equally balanced across the catamaran, the primary rescuers roll the canoe over into an upright position.

9. They slide the canoe into the water and position it parallel to the catamaran, carefully avoiding the swimmers.

10. The primary rescuers hold together the gunwales of the canoes, creating a trimaran, before each swimmer kicks hard to propel herself into the canoe.

Reentering the canoe can sometimes be difficult for women without strong upper bodies. The rescuers can dip the canoe gunwale downward so swimmers can roll in over the lower side. A rescuer also can grab the swimmer's life jacket so she doesn't slide back into the water. I've seen people use a loop of rope or webbing that hooks around the gunwale and drapes over the side of the canoe deep enough for swimmers to get their foot in the loop. The hanging loop gives them a "step" up to roll in over the side.

All river rescues are inherently chaotic because the current keeps pushing you and the canoe downriver. Always look downstream to see if new obstacles require a change in strategy.

Practice these rescues at a safe site with gentle current, no obstacles, and a shoreline free of hazards such as downed trees. Because the current can actually help push the canoe toward shore, it's easier to tow in the boat in a river than on a lake. Sometimes the canoe may spin in the current or on obstacles, and you may find yourself on the downstream end. You'll have to make a decision about whether it's safer to swim away from the canoe, try to turn it by yanking on the safety line, or move to the new upstream end by moving along the upstream side of the canoe. If you cannot make headway, let the canoe go and swim to safety without it. Rescue requires lots of quick decisions, but you develop sound judgment through repeated practice. The ability to self-rescue also develops enormous self-confidence, which ultimately makes you a bolder canoeist.

A **catamaran** stabilizes the rescue while the canoe is emptied of water.

THE ACTIVE RIVER SWIMMER

Once you begin to canoe in swiftly moving rivers, self-rescue becomes even more important if you capsize. Obstacles downstream can be potentially hazardous, but with knowledge and skill, you can rescue yourself quickly and safely. Don't benignly float and expect others to assist you because they may not be in a position to do so. You want to immediately begin your own rescue.

The same rescue priorities apply in the river: people first, then canoes, and finally gear. To enhance your personal safety, follow these guidelines:

- Don't stand up in the river; its power can knock you underwater if your foot gets trapped in rocks.
- Get onto your back, and keep your feet downstream of your body so they (rather than your head) fend off any oncoming obstacles.
- Keep your feet near the surface by kicking so they don't catch in any underwater debris.
- Keep your butt up and lay out flat on your back so your body slides over underwater rocks and ledges.
- If you are downstream of the canoe, immediately swim away from it so it doesn't hit you.
- Check to make sure your partner is okay. Call her by name if you can't see her.
- Determine the safest shoreline (free of obstacles) and swim toward it.
- Hold onto the safety line (and your paddle) about 4 to 5 feet away from the boat and use an aggressive side stroke with strong kicking to swim with the canoe to shore.
- For safety, stay on the upstream end of the canoe.
- Look for other canoes that may be arriving to assist.

current

In a **whitewater self-rescue**, secure both your paddle and the canoe's painter or safety line with one hand. Use your free arm to swim your way to shore.

Deb Williams, 50, a director of the Hulbert Outdoor Centre in Fairlee, Vermont, discovered in a rescue clinic how to swim rapids safely and how to feel comfortable in waterlogged clothing. She said, "Swimming the rapids was exhilarating. I loved it. But it was also frightening. It was like jumping off the high diving board when I was a kid." Her advice is take the plunge; it will feel great when you learn how to do it properly.

GROUP SWIFTWATER RESCUES

Rescuers can help swimmers get to shore when it is safe to do so. That means that swimmers may have to swim through a river section with boulders until they reach a fairly open stretch of water that allows others to assist. All rescuers must be aware of their actions relative to the swimmers, and they must continually look downriver to see if any unforeseen obstacles may interfere with the rescue. The rescuers' primary responsibility is to avoid complicating the rescue scene!

Two basic types of rescues are useful: towing and bumping. *Towing* enables you to paddle in the swimmers and their canoe on your stern safety line. *Bumping* is direct hitting of the capsized craft to push it toward shore. The rescues can be used singly or in combination with each other.

Towing

A boat just upriver can quickly paddle down to the capsized canoe and alert the swimmers of their intent to assist. The rescuers must spin their canoe into position just above the capsized boat, with their bow pointed to the safest shore and the stern just beside the swimmer towing the canoe. You need to be close enough to hand the stern safety line to the swimmer without hitting her as she grabs it. Otherwise, you may not get the safety line in her hand. (The swamped canoe is traveling more swiftly downriver than the spinning rescue boat, which is stopped in the river.)

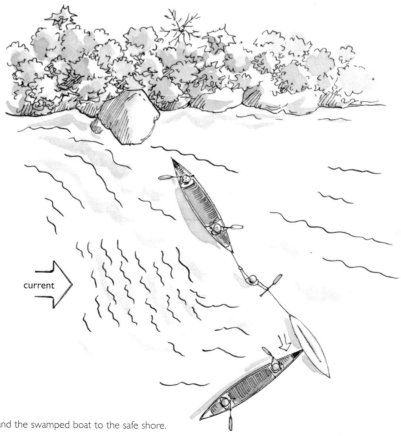

current

Rescue canoes can **tow** and **bump** the paddler and the swamped boat to the safe shore.

• •

"You should never paddle farther from shore than you can swim or self-rescue."

—Becky Mason

• •

Now paddle directly to the safe shore as hard as you can. As soon as the safety line goes taut, the swimmers with their swamped boat will act like an anchor and begin to turn the rescue boat more upriver. You may need to turn the bow of the rescue boat back toward shore; otherwise, you'll just stall out in the river. The key to success here is paddle hard and don't give up! Also, assistance from other canoeists can help shorten the time of the rescue.

Bumping

Once the tow rescue happens, a third canoe can paddle downriver to push the capsized canoe toward shore (see illustration on page 81). The rescue canoe positions itself on the upstream side of the capsized canoe at the approximate midpoint and bumps the canoe quite hard to ram it toward shore. Sometimes the canoe will sink in the river and you may slide up onto it a little; just back off and bump it again. Rescuers may need to adjust their position, sometimes bumping closer to the upstream end of the capsized canoe. Your goal is to keep the canoe angled against the current, rather than aligned with it, so the current continues to push the boat toward shore.

Practice these rescues at a site with mild current and no downstream obstacles. I recommend staying upright at first and focusing on getting into position. The rescue boats will discover that the hardest part is getting close to the "capsized" canoe smoothly and quickly without having to maneuver excessively. You usually have to get closer than you think to actually hand off the safety line. Too much time spent getting into position means the rescue operation floats too far downstream—risking involvement with more hazards.

Once the rescue boats can reach the "distressed" boat quickly, it's time to practice a rescue. Flip over the canoe and let rescuers actually tow and bump the boat to shore. It's quite rewarding to execute such a rescue without relying on outside help, and you'll feel confident about your ability to handle beginning whitewater.

Shoreline rescues

If you think a tricky rapid might tip over a canoe, then your group can establish a safety system along an unobstructed shoreline free of obstacles. You can prepare to assist potential swimmers by setting up a throw-bag rescue. Rescuers position themselves below the rapid, far enough apart so their bags aren't likely to tangle. This assisted rescue

• •

"The mark of a good rescue is one where the swimmers never let go of their paddles. Clutch your paddle as you would your best friend!"

• •

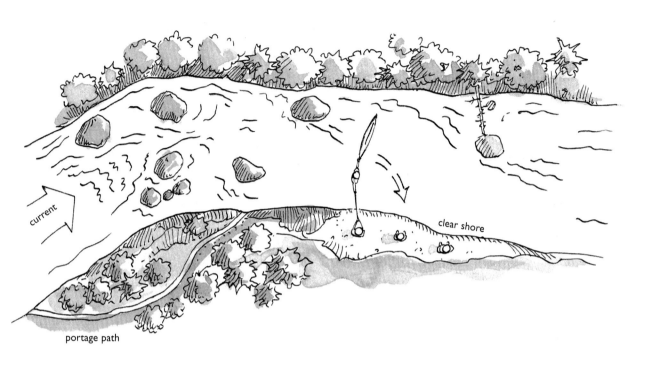

A **shoreline rescue** allows swimmers to swing toward shore on a rescue line.

relies on the swimmer initiating a good self-rescue: she is on her back, upstream of or away from her canoe, and, if possible, moving toward shore by kicking her feet.

The upstream line is thrown first, when a swimmer is directly opposite the rescuer. Call the person's name, and then yell "rope" as the line plays out and extends past the swimmer. Most women find that an underhanded throw, like pitching a softball or rolling a bowling ball, gets the bag the farthest. Wetting the bag makes it heavier so it travels farther, too. Some of the beefier bags are actually quite difficult to throw. I've found that a medium-weight bag works best for me.

Be prepared for a hard tug on the rope once the swimmer grabs onto it, especially if she is holding onto the canoe with the other hand. But don't belay or wrap the rope around your body or a tree, because the swimmer won't be able to continue clasping the rope. Move down the shore a little bit to relieve the pressure, and then let the swimmer swing into the eddy on the end

"**R**emember the rule for any self-rescue: swim to shore, and don't stand up until your buttocks bump on the rocks in shallow water."

of the line. The second and third lines are thrown only if the first fails to reach the swimmer or if the swimmer fails to catch it.

In all rescues, other canoes in the group stand by to assess whether the rescue is happening safely. Then they can rescue any gear that may have floated downriver. The mark of a good rescue is one where the swimmers never let go of their paddles. Clutch your paddle as you would your best friend! (Several manuals on rescue techniques are available; see those listed in chapter 11.)

Chapter 8

GETTING EQUIPPED

Functional paddling gear and clothing has matured since 1897, when ladies sought guidance about appropriate river dress in a little society book called *Manners for Women*. The author, described only as Mrs. Humphrey, advised women that lace-trimmed white petticoats and black patent shoes were quite out of place in a canoe, but she pronounced that some ornamentation of simple, tailor-cut clothing was permissible in one's river costume!

Today, manufacturers have developed canoeing equipment and clothing specifically for the female shape, which makes it more functional than ever for women. No longer is gear simply sized down and painted pink. Companies recognize that female paddlers are often short-waisted, have differently shaped chests, and clasp paddles with smaller hands. That's good news for women who have worn ill-fitting life jackets for years and canoed with paddles too large for their bodies. In fact, women's gear is finally evident in outdoor catalogs because manufacturers have realized that women are an expanding market in paddlesports. We are very willing to buy gear that works well.

You'll be able to test types and styles of gear at instructional schools and outfitters, which is a great place to begin. These companies may have retail shops as well, and the staff, often avid paddlers, are more knowledgeable than most outdoor retail chains. If water is available near the store, ask to test the gear. Even 15 minutes of paddling can help you determine whether a life jacket or a paddle feels comfortable when you execute a stroke.

Freestyle-canoeing champion Karen Knight, who describes herself as "5 feet tall on a good hair day," advises smaller women to explore children's paddling clothing and gear. She finds that kids' stuff can fit well and that a range of good-quality items is available for the entry-level canoeist. However, Karen said companies don't always produce their most technical products in those small sizes. She still has to cut down the grips on her competition paddles so they fit her hands properly. If you are small and want to buy top-quality gear at the beginning, ask your paddling retailer for this service.

SELECTING A PADDLE

One of the easiest purchases is your paddle, which you can tailor to your size and paddling needs quite nicely. The two basic types are *straight-* and *bent-shaft* paddles. A *straight shaft* is versatile and can be used in all types of canoeing; it stores easily at home or in the canoe. The *bent shaft* is a specialized paddle best used on flat-water for touring or marathon racing, and it offers a more efficient forward stroke. The most common angle of 14 degrees between the shaft and the blade keeps the blade vertical throughout the stroke and enhances power. With a straight shaft, the paddle lifts water through a portion of the stroke, which requires more effort. However, a bent-shaft paddle is not as versatile for whitewater paddling because it can be awkward to use with repeated turning strokes.

Paddles are available in a range of materials, which affect price ($17 to $150) and function:

- **Plastic** is inexpensive and durable, but thicker plastics can feel like heavy clubs, and thinner blades can become too flexible with abuse.

- An **aluminum** shaft is light and inexpensive, but it can be cold to grasp.

- **Wood** offers a warm feel and more flexibility if you have joint problems, but it requires more care.

- **Fiberglass** is light and only moderately expensive, but the blade tip can wear away with repeated bashing. Its stiffness can aggravate joint problems.

- **Carbon** is light, stiff, and catches aerated whitewater quite well, but it is expensive.

*A **bent-shaft paddle** is efficient for racing and for flatwater touring.*

Now consider the effect of blade shape and width. The classic style is the *beavertail*, which has a narrow, 6-inch width that allows the paddle to glide smoothly, quietly, and with little resistance through the water. It works well for touring on flatwater. Narrower paddles are best if you have tendinitis or arthritis, because the smaller surface area reduces the amount of resistance against the water that gets transmitted to your joints. If you plan to paddle whitewater, then you want the wider blade of about 8 inches with a squarish tip. Increased width gives the blade more surface area, which in frothy water lets you grab more of it. Recently, canoe paddles have been designed with the *scooped* blade, which helps you lock onto the water solidly at the catch position. Whitewater racers and avid playboaters like this feature, but it's an unnecessary and expensive feature for a recreational canoeist.

The size and shape of the paddle grip can be important for women with smaller hands. The *T grip* on the whitewater paddle allows you to clasp the paddle firmly and angle it more easily during turning strokes; the *palm grip* on the beavertail and bent-shaft paddles minimizes hand fatigue. Whitewater canoeists like the increased control of the T grip; flatwater paddlers like the relaxed palm grip for cruising. However, many women find that the palm grip is so big for their hands that they can't clasp the paddle adequately. The palm grip is preferred by freestyle canoeists, who can rotate the grip smoothly in their palms to execute dramatic and stylish moves with different sides of the blade.

A final consideration is the shaft, because its shape also can affect your comfort. Shafts are changing from the standard, rounder shape to a narrower, oval shape nicer for smaller hands. Paddles advertised specifically as women's models should have this new shape.

palm grip

T grip

A **straight-shaft paddle** is useful for all types of canoeing. A **palm grip** minimizes hand fatigue, whereas a **T grip** offers greater control.

Sizing a paddle

Forget your height in sizing a paddle; legs aren't important when sitting or kneeling in the canoe. Run from any salesperson who tries to measure the paddle from the floor to your chin! The more important measurement is the length of your torso; if you have a shorter torso, you generally need a shorter paddle for tandem paddling.

How do you know what length? Consider your forward stroke: When the blade is fully immersed in the water, the grip should reach to your nose. That's fine, but approximating that length is hard in the retail store when you can't put a paddle to water. Here is what you can do:

1. Kneel down on the floor and raise your butt to its approximate level on a canoe seat (about 8 inches off the floor, although seat height will vary somewhat by type of boat).

2. Invert the paddle and put the grip on the floor.

3. The throat of the blade should reach to your chin or nose.

4. Some paddle manufacturers use a sizing chart that measures the length of your torso (from a sitting position) to your nose. However, I've found that the recommended paddle lengths often run short for me, even though I have a very short torso. The best approach is to paddle a variety of lengths to see which feels best with forward strokes.

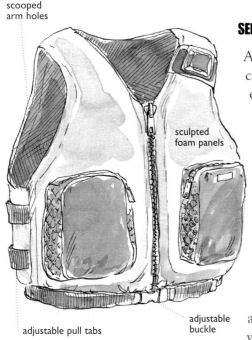

scooped
arm holes

sculpted
foam panels

adjustable
buckle

adjustable pull tabs

A **PFD** designed for women can be cinched tightly yet comfortably.

SELECTING A LIFE VEST

A *life vest* or *personal flotation device* (PFD) is essential for canoeing safely, and it must fit securely and comfortably to be effective. The best PFDs are pullover styles that can be cinched tightly with side and waist straps, because they won't slide up when you float in water. Most models found in paddlesport shops are very functional U.S. Coast Guard Type III jackets designed for recreational boating that, at a minimum, must give you 15.5 pounds of flotation or buoyancy. If you want increased flotation to keep your head higher above the water, then choose a model with more foam in the chest or shoulder area or in an extra band below your waist strap. Heavier women may appreciate this extra security.

"*Always* wear a life jacket," advises Candace Rapf, 51, a school nurse from Amherst, New Hampshire. "Make sure you purchase one that fits and isn't too long (it will ride up when you sit) or uncomfortable. If it's uncomfortable, there will be the temptation not to put it on. . . . My life is too important to mess around without it, and I care too much about the people I'm with to subject them to all that would occur if I drowned because I was too foolish to wear one. . . . It's great for warmth around a campsite, too."

Test the buoyancy in a PFD by floating in shallow water, relaxing your body, and letting your head tilt back. Your chin should be free of the water so you can breathe easily. If you can't do this, then you need a PFD with additional foam, primarily in the front, to keep your face away from the water.

Some companies produce leg straps that can be purchased separately and added to the life vest. The straps prevent a life vest from being pulled from your body, but they must be fitted closely to the body to avoid snagging on objects. They provide a secure fit for small children, for people with a disability that makes it hard to secure a life jacket, and for women whose stomach or waist measurement is greater than their chest measurement, particularly during pregnancy.

Features appreciated by women are deeper, scooped armholes that reduce chafing, softer foam in the front panels that molds to the shape of your breasts, and shorter lengths that suit short torsos. Recent models use neoprene at the armholes and shoulders for a softer fit against the body.

The styles today are contoured to a woman's shape. Heidi Krantz, 40, a co-owner of Umiak Outfitters in Stowe, Vermont, remembers the stiff styles of the past: "I always felt like a turtle in the old vests. I would turn my body, and the vest would stay still like a turtle shell. Now there is incredible freedom of movement."

Often the only way to keep a vest tight enough to not loosen in the water was to cinch it "until you felt like a sausage casing," said Kristin Peterson, 40, of Northfield, Massachusetts. "With the new vests my cleavage isn't up under my chin. It's down where it should be!"

If you plan to invest in only one paddling item, make it a life vest. Prices range from $44 to $100, but it's a good investment in your paddling comfort and safety. Test the overall fit by asking a friend to pull up on the PFD after you have tightened all straps. It should not slide up and obscure your face.

grab loop

flotation collar

adjustable buckle

leg straps

OUTFITTING YOUR CHILD WITH A PFD
• • • • • • • • • • • • • • • • • •

Life vests are available for infants, toddlers, and youth and have the primary goal of providing high flotation and head support. A collar of flotation is added to the PFD for the youngest, and the distribution of foam (more in the front panels, little or no panels in the back) is designed to turn the child face up in the water. However, children tend to struggle in the water, so the PFD cannot prevent them from flipping face down if they panic. A grab loop at the collar allows you to lift them quickly from the water.

Older children can benefit from a junior-sized jacket that is extremely adjustable. Designed to accommodate the growth years, this vest can offer as much as 10 inches of expansion and as many as four straps of adjustment on the side to cinch it in tightly. Women who weigh 90 to 100 pounds should explore the junior models.

A **flotation collar** helps float a child's relatively heavy head.

SELECTING A CANOE

Once you discover that canoeing must be a regular part of your lifestyle, then it's time to purchase a boat. Whether you seek a lightweight canoe or a durable boat that your kids can clamber on, you can find it among the more than 1,000 models of canoes available for sale. Your purpose for canoeing will affect what type of boat to purchase.

Let's examine more closely the basic flatwater and whitewater types, originally introduced in chapter 4, so that you can compare different characteristics. I've included more detailed descriptions of the basic models so that you understand their function:

- **Flatwater Touring:** a faster, longer boat that covers distances on gentle water with minimal paddling effort; enough cargo capacity for overnight camping.

- **Freestyle:** a shorter, maneuverable boat that can be leaned dramatically in special stunts.

- **Marathon Racing:** a long, streamlined canoe that tracks exceptionally well with a shallow depth to minimize wind resistance.

- **General Whitewater:** a durable boat that can track and turn moderately well; a general-purpose boat that also can be used on flatwater.

- **Whitewater Touring:** a longer, durable canoe that can track well through rapids; has a greater depth to shed waves and store overnight gear.

- **Whitewater Play:** a shorter, durable canoe with rockered ends that is easy to maneuver amid challenging features in the river.

- **Rodeo:** a short, highly rockered boat filled with flotation that can spin quickly and surf waves in the river.

The shape of the *hull* (main body of the canoe stripped of any parts) affects a boat's stability. A canoe with *initial stability* is usually flat-bottomed and most stable in flatwater; its sides are often straight or have *tumblehome* (an inward curvature just below the gunwale)—and these shapes don't provide much security when the boat is leaned. But many women find that this narrower boat width lets them get their paddle in the water more easily. A canoe with *secondary stability* usually has a V-shaped bottom or flared sides and is stable when leaned on its side (to one side of the V).

Canoes can be made from a variety of materials, which affects weight, cost, and performance. You can find inexpensive and lightweight *aluminum* canoes—some crafted right after World War II—that are still quite functional for flatwater paddling (although probably quite dented!). Traditionally crafted canoes are beautifully constructed of *wood* with an outer canvas or fiberglass layer and require careful handling, so they are best used on flatwater. Also suitable for

CANOE TYPES AND CHARACTERISTICS

TYPE	LENGTH	TRACKING	TURNING	STABILITY	DRYNESS	VOLUME
Flatwater Touring	Tandem, 17' Solo, 13'	High	Low	Initial	Medium	Medium or High
Freestyle	Tandem, 15' Solo, 13'	Medium	Medium	Secondary	Medium	Low or Medium
Marathon Racing	Tandem, 18'6" Solo, 17'6"	Extremely High	Extremely Low	Initial	Low	Low
General Whitewater	Tandem, 16' Solo, 13'	Medium	Medium	Initial or Secondary	Medium	Medium
Whitewater Touring	Tandem, 17' Solo, 15'	High	Low	Initial or Secondary	High	High
Whitewater Play	Tandem, 15' Solo, 12'	Low	High	Secondary	Medium	Medium
Rodeo	Solo, 10'6"	Extremely Low	Extremely High	Secondary	High	Medium

Canoe lengths are approximate. Some models may vary 6 inches or more from the lengths listed here.

calm water is a *fiberglass* canoe, made from layers of cloth impregnated with resin that create a rigid shape in a moderately heavy canoe. A fiberglass canoe is only moderately expensive and easy to repair, but it can abrade or crack on contact with rocks.

The lightest weight is *Kevlar* construction, another type of cloth filled with resin that creates a strong, efficient hull. Kevlar cloth is about half the weight of fiberglass, yet it is stronger. You can paddle a Kevlar canoe with minimal effort and, because it is the same material found in bulletproof vests, the cloth is more tear- and puncture-resistant. You can readily lift a Kevlar canoe onto your car rack, but expect to pay a high price for this feature. It is found in both flatwater and white-water canoes.

Durability is a desired trait in whitewater canoes, and plastic canoes perform quite well because they slip over obstacles easily. Two general types of plastic canoes are manufactured: *poly-ethylene*, in which molten beads of plastic are fired in a canoe mold in a large oven; and *acrylonitrile butadiene-styrene (ABS)*, which is a sheet of foam sandwiched between two sheets of plastic.

Foldable canoes are light, portable, and maneuverable.

A huge, hot press shapes the ABS laminate over an overturned canoe mold, almost like a pair of pants pressed at the cleaners! The polyethylene boats are cheaper to make, and the savings gets passed along to the consumer. You won't mind dragging this canoe up onto the beach. The hull of an ABS canoe can be shaped more readily for higher performance, which makes it more expensive. The plastic outer layer also doesn't abrade as much as polyethylene, which gets a scuffed look over time and moves more slowly through the water due to its rough surface. Plastic canoes are lowest in maintenance, but they are not light, and the more flexible hull in some models can take more effort to paddle.

Foldable canoes, a type of skin-frame construction, offer women a nice lightweight option in solo and tandem models. A plastic vinyl skin stretches tightly around an aluminum frame; flotation baffles tightly secured between the frame and the skin give the canoe hull some rigidity. Based on the folding principles of a sea kayak, these canoes can be easily stored or transported in a bundle as small as a duffel bag. The flexible frame allows the canoe to ride easily up over waves in whitewater and stay quite dry. Although the skin can tear, the material is easy to repair with fast-drying patches.

The "Canoe Materials" table on page 93 provides a general range of prices and weights of canoes produced by some of the larger manufacturing companies. Generally the lighter the boat, the heftier the price. You must realize that canoe weight can vary greatly depending on length and details of construction. For instance, fiberglass and Kevlar cloth are produced in various weights and weaves. They can be interwoven with other fibers and layered lightly or heavily, which also affects durability. For more specific information by model, the best sources are the annual *Buyer's Guide* issues published each winter by *Canoe & Kayak* and *Paddler* magazines. They list almost 1,000 canoe models produced by approximately 100 manufacturers.

Buying a used canoe is an excellent way to acquire a canoe inexpensively. Check the bulletin boards at paddle shops, marinas, and outdoor stores to tap into the lively trade in used boats. You can often find a very functional boat for flatwater for less than $400. It's harder to find such good deals on higher-performance boats, which are more expensive out of the factory, but you can find discounted boats. Some canoe manufacturers also have end-of-season sales to gain warehouse space for next year's models. Also, ask for boats that are considered "seconds," but check the reason for the imperfection. It might be that the canoe only has cosmetic imperfections, which don't affect boat function. Some plastic boats will be considered "blemished" if the layers of plastic are

CANOE MATERIALS

MATERIAL	TYPE	COST	WEIGHT (LBS.)	BENEFITS
Aluminum	Tandem	$200 used	60–85	Low-maintenance
	Solo		50–70	
Wood	Tandem	$3,300–3,500	75–105	Aesthetic
	Solo	$3,000–3,300	65–75	
Fiberglass	Tandem	$720–1,200	65–70	Lightweight
	Solo	$600–700	30–55	Easy to repair
Kevlar	Tandem	$1,500–2,500	40–50	Very lightweight
	Solo	$1,000–$1,600	25–55	Puncture resistant
Polyethylene	Tandem	$730–1,000	80–85	Low-maintenance
	Solo	$500–760	45–75	Inexpensive
ABS	Tandem	$1,200–1,400	70–80	Durable
	Solo	$950–1,100	45–60	

thicker than advertised; the canoe will weigh more than a normal model, but that does make it more durable.

Mary McClintock, of Conway, Massachusetts, suggests that a canoe co-op is a good way to keep the activity affordable. Buy equipment with another friend or small group of friends. The purchases are cheaper, and the gear gets used more frequently.

OUTFITTING YOUR CANOE

I once stepped into a friend's boat to paddle it down a rapid she wanted to skip that day, and I felt like I had walked into her house! The canoe was customized to her particular style, which was different than mine. Each boat tends to take on the character of its owner. You can outfit your canoe for safety and comfort in some simple ways.

All boats need *safety lines* tied to the bow and stern, and the best material is bright yellow polypropylene rope. It floats and is easy to spot. I cut the lines so they stretch at least three quarters of the canoe length after they are tied on. That length gives me enough to tie the canoe onto my car. Most importantly, if I've capsized, I can get my body well away from the boat and see upcoming obstacles while still holding onto a good amount of line.

A **yoke thwart** lets you carry the canoe alone.

A *padded portage yoke* in place of a center thwart is a useful feature on a canoe. These contoured yokes fit nicely around the shoulders; even if you don't plan to tackle long trips with portages, they are helpful for moving the canoe from your car rack to the water. Because women's shoulders slope downward more than men's, I've found that additional closed-cell foam from a sleeping pad can be glued onto the wood thwart for a better and more comfortable fit.

Whitewater paddlers need to outfit their canoes with flotation to make rescue easier. *Air bags* tied into the canoe and secured under a latticework of cord displace water and help the canoe float higher and free of obstacles. You can pull it more easily to shore as well. *Kneepads* glued to the canoe bottom will save tender joints, and they eliminate the discomfort that can occur by wearing athletic pads that bind behind the knee. I also have tied *loose cord loops* around my stern and bow thwarts so I can buckle in a rescue throw bag, first-aid kit, and waterproof bag with extra clothing and food. In general, I don't tie in large packs and dry bags, because they interfere with T rescues. Properly waterproofed, the gear will float on the lake or collect in river eddies for pickup after the rescue ends.

safety line
flotation bag
flotation bag
safety line
restraint cords

Flotation is important in whitewater play canoes to displace water if you tip over.

YOUR CANOEING CLOSET

Personal preparedness is important for handling the climate—a big factor in paddling that can affect your safety and comfort. Think function rather than fashion in selecting clothing; treat what you wear as safety gear. While you can invest in some of the nifty paddlesport fashions currently available, you also can scrounge most items from your closet rather cheaply.

Canoeists must be aware of *hypothermia*, which occurs when the body temperature drops below normal; immersion in cold water only aggravates the condition. Cold, wet conditions, particularly when the wind kicks up, can cause you to shiver, become clumsy, and in the worst stage, lose judgment and consciousness. Hypothermia can occur in any season, but spring is a particularly vulnerable time for paddlers. The air temperature may be quite warm, but the water temperature is still in the 40s—definitely cold enough to make you gasp when the canoe overturns. Above all, think about preventing hypothermia, and dress for the water in clothing that will keep you warm while wet. Even the splash from your paddle can be chilling on a cold day.

Cold-weather protection

Use the basic principles of layering for the outdoors in selecting your clothing, adjusting clothing for your body type and metabolism and the water temperature. When the water dips below 60°F, you want to be fully protected from the cold. In spring whitewater in New England, I wear medium-weight polypropylene long underwear, a fleece vest that adds an insulating layer, and a drysuit. Avoid cotton, which provides no warmth; wool does provide warmth when wet, but it can feel heavy. Wring it out to avoid that water-logged feeling.

The *drysuit* shown here is a coated nylon, one-piece suit with rubber gaskets at the neck, wrists, and ankles that prevent water from entering the suit. You slither into it and zip it up with a heavy-duty, waterproof zipper across the chest. Because I tend to run warm, I usually have to dip into the river on a sunny day to cool off; otherwise,

COLD-WEATHER PREPAREDNESS

- Polypropylene long underwear
- Fleece vest or pullover
- Wetsuit/paddling jacket or drysuit
- Wool or fleece hat
- Neoprene booties or sock/boot combo
- Mitts or pogies
- Sunglasses
- Sunscreen
- Thermos with hot drinks
- High-energy snacks and lunch
- Extra insulating layers in a waterproof sack

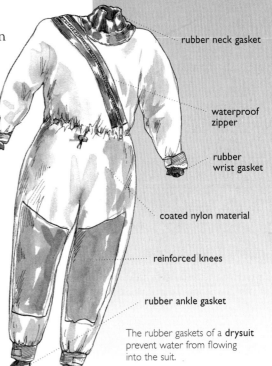

rubber neck gasket

waterproof zipper

rubber wrist gasket

coated nylon material

reinforced knees

rubber ankle gasket

The rubber gaskets of a **drysuit** prevent water from flowing into the suit.

WARM-WEATHER PREPAREDNESS

· · · · · · · · · · · · · · · ·

- Bathing suit
- Quick-drying nylon shorts
- Short- and long-sleeved shirts for sun protection
- Sunglasses
- Brimmed hat
- Sandals or rubber boots
- Sunscreen
- At least 2 liters of water per person
- Nylon windbreaker
- Snacks and lunch
- Extra clothing, including rain gear, in a waterproof sack

I create a little sauna inside the suit from perspiration. Drysuits are the most expensive option ($200 to $600), but they are warm. Invest in a drop-seat zipper to make "bathroom" breaks easier.

An alternative to a drysuit is a neoprene *wetsuit*, which operates on the principle of warming the layer of water (perspiration) next to your skin. The most popular model is an overall style called a "Farmer John," which leaves your arms uncovered and mobile. Prices begin at $65 for a front-zipper model; buy the ones with full leg lengths because your legs will be exposed to wind and splash. Canoeists often use a wetsuit with a nylon paddling jacket as the outer layer, under which they wear the usual layers of synthetic clothing. Jacket prices begin at $75.

As the weather warms up, canoeists begin to modify the basic drysuit or wetsuit system. They may cover their insulating layers with nylon paddling pants and continue to use a paddling jacket, which still minimizes the shock if they swim. A rainsuit also works well, but avoid ponchos or *cagoules* (long raincoats), which are cumbersome if you capsize.

Women with poor circulation may like the *pogie*. These are nylon shells in the shape of a mitt that fit over your hands as they grasp the paddle. I like them better than gloves, in which I feel like I can't get a firm grip on the paddle. Playtex dishwashing gloves will break the wind and provide a good grasp at a much cheaper price.

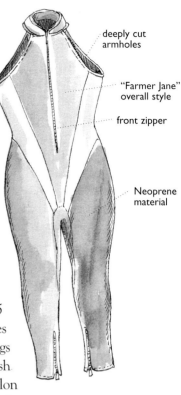

deeply cut armholes

"Farmer Jane" overall style

front zipper

Neoprene material

A **wetsuit** is a cheaper alternative in cold weather.

Nylon **pogies** protect your hands from wind and water.

Neoprene booties ($50) keep your feet warm. Choose a model with a thick sole to protect you from the broken glass commonly found at put-ins. Wool or polypropylene socks with old boots and sneakers work well with less expense.

Warm-weather protection

Hyperthermia occurs when your body temperature rises above normal, and it is usually aggravated by dehydration. This condition is simpler to prevent while paddling because you can slip over the side to cool down. Bring plenty of water to drink—at least two liters or more.

The sun strikes a canoeist in two ways: directly from above and reflected from below, off the water. Getting sunburned under your chin is a possibility! Protect yourself with lightweight clothing that dries easily (cotton is just fine in summer), a fully brimmed hat that protects the ears, and sunscreen liberally applied to your face, neck, and backs of your hands. A good lip balm prevents chapped lips. Sunglasses with UV protection are wise, and polarized lenses cut the glare off the water. Wearing sunglasses also helps prevent headaches.

SAFETY EQUIPMENT AND ACCESSORIES

Beyond the wearing of a life jacket, you can purchase other items that enhance your personal safety or that of your canoe group. Carry these items in the canoe on any excursion, day-long or multiday.

A whistle attached to your life jacket is a good signaling device in the event of an emergency. Three long blasts is an international sign of distress, usually when a life is threatened, and it alerts the group to a real emergency. A whistle blast is the signal to other canoeists to render assistance appropriate to the situation. Some groups also like to use a chirping signal to communicate across water, which is also a recognized international signal. However, I've never felt comfortable using a whistle simply to get someone's attention; my groups save the whistle for a real emergency.

The rescue throw bag is necessary for river trips in swift water. These quick-throw bags (from $45 to $50) have bright yellow or orange polypropylene line that floats on the water. A rescuer standing on shore throws the bag to a canoeist who has capsized and holds the line to swing the swimmer into shore. Usually

SAFETY GEAR AND ACCESSORIES

- Whistle
- Rescue throw bag (whitewater)
- Helmet (whitewater)
- First-aid kit
- Extra food
- Extra paddles
- Matches
- Map and compass
- Small sheathed or folding knife

FIRST-AID KIT CHECKLIST

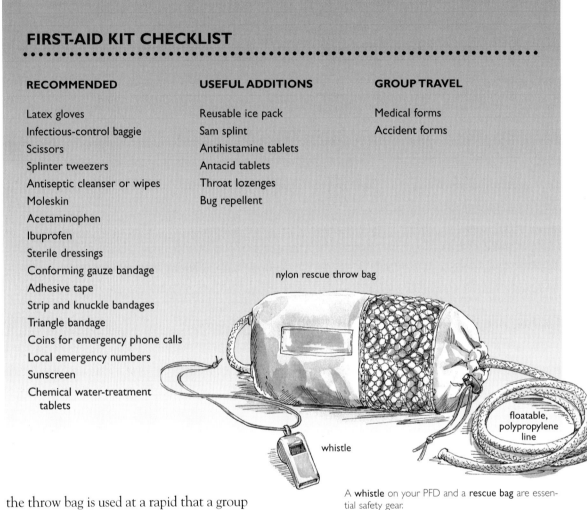

RECOMMENDED

Latex gloves
Infectious-control baggie
Scissors
Splinter tweezers
Antiseptic cleanser or wipes
Moleskin
Acetaminophen
Ibuprofen
Sterile dressings
Conforming gauze bandage
Adhesive tape
Strip and knuckle bandages
Triangle bandage
Coins for emergency phone calls
Local emergency numbers
Sunscreen
Chemical water-treatment
    tablets

USEFUL ADDITIONS

Reusable ice pack
Sam splint
Antihistamine tablets
Antacid tablets
Throat lozenges
Bug repellent

GROUP TRAVEL

Medical forms
Accident forms

nylon rescue throw bag

floatable, polypropylene line

whistle

A **whistle** on your PFD and a **rescue bag** are essential safety gear.

the throw bag is used at a rapid that a group has scouted and determined might cause a spill. The best way for a woman to throw a rescue bag is with an underhand swing, like pitching a softball or rolling a bowling ball. Wetting the bag first also makes it heavier and helps it travel farther.

Helmets are necessary for whitewater travel if you intend to adopt a playful style of canoeing. Your chances of capsizing increase if you turn in and out of eddies and play in waves. Most canoeists don't wear helmets if they are simply traveling straight downriver on a trip in a conservative fashion. The helmets shown on page 99 ($45 to $60) are made from high-impact-resistant plastic with an internal foam liner to protect your head. Some outer shells extend downward around the ears for increased protection. When fitted properly, the helmet should cover your forehead. Don't wear one beanie-style on the back of your head!

A first-aid kit tailored to your medical skills is a sound idea, and it also should be geared to the paddling environment. Most accidents happen on shore at launch sites, where canoeists can encounter broken glass, fish hooks, and additional residue from other users. The majority of first-aid situations are minor cuts, abrasions, and blisters. Tender hands unused to holding a paddle may suffer from blisters, so plenty of moleskin backed up by adhesive tape should be included. You can spend $40 to $90 for a commercial waterproofed kit with contents, but it may be more than your skills can handle. Building your own kit is easy and usually cheaper because you can stock it from items already in your home.

A **helmet** protects your head if you capsize in whitewater. Some models provide ear protection, as well.

Finally, knowing basic first aid and cardiopulmonary resuscitation (CPR) is always a good idea because a natural result of canoeing on rivers and lakes is that you will most likely be unable to reach medical support quickly.

TLC FOR YOUR GEAR

Rivers and lakes aren't always the cleanest, especially stillwater areas in late summer, so washing out your personal gear is a good investment to prolong its life. Your perspiration combined with sunscreen and bug repellent is a powerful mix, and it can weaken fabrics if left to fester. Simply rinsing out nylon, other laminated fabrics, and neoprene items after each use is effective. Several times a year, I also soak these items in the bathtub with a gentle powdered soap. Neoprene booties and socks can get especially disgusting—I wash them in the washing machine on the gentle cycle with no ill effects.

Always dry your gear thoroughly so it doesn't mildew, and hang it up away from the sun. Regularly treat drysuit gaskets with 303 Protectant so the rubber stays supple. You can replace the gaskets on these suits, but at a hefty price. Waterproof treatments of nylon paddling jackets, pants, and raincoats are helpful in prolonging their performance. Products like Scotchguard have versions specially designed for the treatment of outdoor clothing.

Throw bags are best dried by unraveling the rope and restuffing it only after it is completely dry. An extremely diluted solution of bleach can eliminate the beasties created by a forgotten snack in any dry bags.

Protecting your paddle

I hang my paddles by their grips on a rack nailed to the porch wall rather than piling them in a corner. Hanging them prevents the tips from getting ground into the cement floor. I also use a fleece paddle cover to protect an expensive carbon paddle; it acts like a beacon to remind me that my top investment is nearby!

If you get a nick on a wooden grip or shaft, you can gently sand the spot with fine-grit sand-paper to get rid of that potential blister site. I also have wound black plastic tape tightly around wooden or fiberglass shafts to prevent damage because I tend to lever my paddle shaft off the gun-wale. The tape takes the brunt; if it wears or tears, I just replace the layer of tape—the shaft never gets touched.

Check wood paddles throughout the season for any cracks or delaminations of the thin fiberglass layer. You may need to reglue the paddle, coat it with varnish, or add a layer of resin to reattach the fiberglass.

Caring for canoes

The sun can be very destructive by weakening plastics and composite materials, so store your canoe out of the sun. If you don't have access to a garage or tree-shaded spot, then throw a tarp over any canoe left in strong sunlight. Be aware that porcupines are attracted to wood gunwales and seats, as we discovered on the Moisie River in Quebec. Whether it was the salt in our per-spiration or glue in the gunwales, the porcupines kept dodging our night watch in an attempt to gnaw the wood.

The best storage position is upside down with the gunwales resting on supports that lift the canoe from the ground. A plastic canoe left on its hull on the ground will begin to sag or flatten out. Hanging it by the safety lines will have the same effect, but I've seen wooden slats very effec-tively suspended by ropes, with the canoe resting on the slats. Wooden gunwales left on the ground will begin to rot.

Plastic boats get stiffer with age and can crack under cold conditions. Check your older canoe carefully, especially after you've hit any obstacles. We applied fiberglass patches on plastic canoes that cracked on a wilderness trip, but it was difficult to do in cold conditions and didn't inspire confidence in the canoes for the remainder of the trip!

Washing canoes free of sand is always a good idea so the sand doesn't get ground into the interior, regardless of the type of material. Each year, I sand the wooden gunwales to keep ahead of splinters. I also apply a light coating of linseed oil to prevent the wood from drying out and cracking. I'd like to say I do this at the beginning and end of each season, but I don't. You should, though!

If you need to perform repairs on boats, get advice from your local boat shop or the manufac-turer. You can easily do fiberglass repairs yourself with guidance from an experienced person; however, repairs of plastic boats, which may involve plastic welding, are more difficult— but not impossible.

Chapter 9

THE CANOE TRIP

I have a favorite canoe trip near my home on the French King Gorge section of the Connecticut River in Massachusetts that we paddle in all weather and seasons. Even a sunny day and open water in January tempt me to get in some irresistible paddling strokes. I like watching the river adapt to the seasons and change its colors.

A canoe trip can be a remote Arctic experience or a "backyard" paddle.

In May, the lacy white shad bush appears stark against the bare trees and heralds the return of shad and salmon in June. During the summer, the increase in noisy jet skis forces me out early in the morning as the valley fog lifts from a silent, green river. By October, leaf-peeping tourists peer down 110 feet from the French King Bridge to watch us slide past steep ledges dotted with scarlet cardinal flowers that match the surrounding maple trees. Then I paddle in the surrealism of snow squalls, where the snow reflects in the water and I feel like Alice in Wonderland paddling through a looking glass.

This backyard trip is not particularly remote. It's not about what author Robert Kimber in *The Canoeist's Sketchbook* calls *mile-bagging*—"a bad habit that quantitatively minded Western

> "**C**anoeing is where I put my head back together."
>
> —Kay Henry, owner, Mad River
> Canoe Company, Vermont

Man is prone to get into." It's about eating a ripe peach alone on a gravel bar after a brisk afternoon paddle. It's about canoeing only a mile to an island camp with a friend trying to overcome a horrible first camping experience, or midday snoozes under idyllic cottonwoods to experience Kimber's feeling of sunny "cooked-through comfort."

Kay Henry, owner of Mad River Canoe Company in Vermont, still tries to complete a wilderness trip every two years, despite managing a busy canoe manufacturing company. She describes her need for canoe trips this way: "Canoeing is where I put my head back together. Water is calming—a repetitive motion that is a pleasant motion. Your thoughts will wander, and it slows you down to a different pace. You don't have to go that far away to be truly 'gone.'"

Where and why do other women enjoy canoe trips? Here are some thoughts:

- "There is a pond in the northern woods of Maine that we visit each year. Here I find peace and solitude." Nancy Reitze, Earthways guide, Canaan, Maine

- "The Yukon is a textured river—it boils, it churns, it swirls. It may be rapidless, but you could hardly call it flat. Its dirty white color derives from the glacial silt dumped in by the White River, and that silt is so fine it is rumored to stay in suspension, without settling out, all the way to the Pacific. There is a magic that derives from the not-so-subtle mix of spectacular scenery, days without nights, and pure air. These are good memories." Call Me Anonymous

- "The Boundary Waters Canoe Area. It's wilderness and very restorative to the soul." Pat Bell, 66, Eden Prairie, Minnesota, author of *Roughing It Elegantly: A Practical Guide to Canoe Camping,* who continues to canoe after hip-replacement surgery (both hips)

- "One special trip for me was the Rio Grande [in Texas] because it was the first time I had slept outdoors on the ground—no tent—and I could watch changes in the sky. Fascinating!" Jean McIntyre, 64, Lyme, New Hampshire

- "The lakes in our town where we go to fish evenings and weekends and stretches of rapids on the Black, Lamoille, and Clyde rivers [in Vermont]. They're special because we go there often and develop the familiarity it takes to recognize little changes, what different water levels do to change the rapids, the comings and goings of wildlife through the seasons." Ann Ingerson, 42, college teacher, Craftsbury, Vermont

- "One special place is the north shore of Lake Superior . . . the absolutely clear water, the clean beaches of pebbles or sand, and the beach environment. There were beautiful days, foggy days, windy days when we'd admire the waves and whitecaps from shore. Lots of birds, even moose." Marge Shepardson, 51, teacher, Marlborough, New Hampshire

● "Two weeks without civilization is a tonic for the soul." Call Me Anonymous

I also love canoe trips because the boat carries the weight. Now, I have been known to backpack (usually with some whining), but I much prefer to travel with my gear stored in a canoe. Why plan a spartan tour by foot, anxiously adding up the pounds of food, clothing, and shelter, when I can canoe in comfort? I learned at the elbow of a pro—my mother, Torry Gullion—who believed that no canoeing trip was complete unless sour cream accompanied the baked potatoes and salad greens balanced a rare steak.

It helps to pick your companions wisely, delegate tasks, and develop some endearing rituals. On cold-weather excursions, my paddling buddy Mary McClintock regularly provides the to-die-for lemon-ginger scones from our favorite local bakery, and I bring the hot herb tea for consumption at our turnaround point. The degree-of-comfort factor is a key point to discuss before embarking on a trip, even among the best of friends.

This chapter includes my tips to plan the trip of your dreams, whether it's on a nearby river or at a remote, more exotic location. The principles of safe and enjoyable tripping are the same, regardless of location and duration. An orientation to river features also is included, as well as some strategies for route-finding on lakes and rivers.

GETTING ORGANIZED

I'm a list-making fool who rarely forgets important items on canoe trips and who can withstand endless kidding from my sister about my clipboard. Be organized and use the checklists in this section during the planning phase and actual execution of the trip. You need to account for

● Realistic self- and group-evaluation

● Route research

● Understanding the local climate and weather

● Permit/access clearance

Begin by honestly evaluating your abilities and personal needs as well as those of other group members. Be in as good physical and mental condition as you can, and adjust for skills impaired by health or conditioning problems. The selected river or lake should be within the paddling ability and fitness level of the least-skilled paddler in the group. Can your group handle an open lake with no wind breaks behind islands or peninsulas? How many miles an hour can people paddle? For how long? A skilled recreational paddler can paddle approximately 3 mph without a break, but speed drops sharply with inexperience, lack of conditioning, and gear in the canoe. I have taken an afternoon to paddle only 1 mile with junior-high kids more interested in swimming than canoeing, but it was a fun mile! And they would willingly paddle again to these favorite ledges for endless acrobatic jumps.

The next step is specific route research. Begin with regional paddling guidebooks—which are plentiful in local bookstores—to read route descriptions. Know the International Scale of River Difficulty established by American Whitewater so that you understand the ratings in the guidebooks (see sidebar, pages 106–7). Then seek out employees at local paddling stores to obtain additional trip information and updates on river conditions. They usually know whether recent storms have changed the river's character and created any hazards, such as downed trees.

Once you've completed this initial fact-finding, consider a route appropriate for your group's skill level. Also check access points in advance, which is important in the event that you need to stop the trip because of illness or injury. Determine how quickly your group can get to them, and then you'll know whether the route will work if a problem arises. Other useful sources of information include automobile travel clubs, local chambers of commerce, local weather services, road atlases, topographical maps, national paddling organizations in other countries, and Internet sites, including paddlers' chat groups (see the resources listed in chapter 11).

Understanding the local environment, such as the climate, is an important part of route research. Be familiar with prevailing weather patterns in the area, particularly the likely wind direction and storm systems. The prevailing winds will tell you which lake shore is likely to be the most protected and, therefore, the most desirable in terms of a route. In Massachusetts, our weather generally comes from a west-northwest direction, so I often check weather reports for the Albany, New York, area to know what is coming our way.

Wind is the canoeist's enemy and, because it tends to build midday, you may find it easier to paddle early and late in the day under calmer conditions. Sometimes on an out-and-back trip, I deliberately paddle into the wind so I can ride tailwinds back to the car. But the insidiousness of shifting winds seems to thwart that strategy much of the time! In some areas, thunderstorms are a regular mid-afternoon phenomenon that can affect your schedule and mileage total. The impact of rain can be considerable on rivers with large watersheds, where feeder streams raise the water levels dramatically. Also be aware that power companies can release water through dams with little notice, changing river levels—up or down—by several feet! I once canoed on a New Hampshire river that faded to a trickle without warning, and we had to portage the boats to shore across damp rocks.

The next step is permit or access clearance. Your chosen river may be subject to permit control since public officials have restricted the number of paddlers on some highly used rivers that flow across federal lands. River access also may be prohibited by private landowners or at public boat ramps designed for powerboat access. If you plan to paddle designated waterways like the Boundary Waters Canoe Area, your outfitter often will arrange the permit for you. Permits may or may not require a fee. Penalties for the lack of a permit can be as high as $500; be aware that some agencies are enforcing the permit rule more strictly today. Honor the system, particularly on private land, and always check to see if it's okay to camp overnight, even if the land isn't posted. We don't want to lose river access and camping privileges, and landowners appreciate those paddlers who ask permission. I've had great responses from owners, even camping with groups, when we promise to use "no-trace" travel practices.

ROUTE-FINDING ON LARGE LAKES

Some of my trickiest paddling has been on the large lakes of the Northwest Territories of Canada because the low-lying tundra gets scoured by winds from the north. A long lake with a north-south orientation, such as Lake Champlain in New York and Vermont, can keep you exposed to tiring headwinds. Crossing from the eastern to western shore requires calm conditions because the wind can build big waves that swamp packed canoes.

The best lakes have an irregular shoreline where peninsulas break the wind. Islands also offer useful protection if you need to make a long crossing, even across a big bay, and new paddlers will welcome the rest breaks. If you know the prevailing winds come from the north, you can select the *lee* shore on the north with reasonable confidence that you'll be protected, as shown for Boat 1 in the illustration at right. If you select the southern shore, you have to be prepared for the possibility that wind-driven waves against this shore can make paddling more chal-

Follow a lee shore for protection against the wind (**Boat 1**), or learn how to ferry against wind currents to make headway (**Boat 2**).

lenging. However, always check local forecasts and know how to read changes in the clouds and wind to determine whether a storm is coming from the south, as they can in New England. Weather radios generally don't work on inland waterways unless you are near the coast.

Tactics used by whitewater canoeists and sailors can be useful on lakes to handle the wind.

INTERNATIONAL SCALE OF RIVER DIFFICULTY

• • • • • • • • • • • • • • • • •

This system is not exact, and regional differences may exist in the rating of whitewater. A river entirely rated at a high level is much more demanding than a river stretch with a few difficult rapids. Also realize that you'll need a bigger margin for safety in cold weather and in remote, inaccessible locations. American Whitewater's difficulty classes for canoes are summarized as follows (the complete descriptions are available from the AWA):

- *Class I:* **Easy.** Fast-moving water with riffles and small waves. Few obstructions, easily avoided with little training.

- *Class II:* **Novice.** Straightforward rapids with wide, clear channels evident without scouting. Occasional maneuvering required, but waves and rocks easily missed by trained canoeists. Group assistance with rescues seldom needed.

- *Class III:* **Intermediate.** Rapids with moderate, irregular waves that can be difficult to avoid and can swamp a canoe. Complex maneuvers in fast current and good

(continued on page 107)

The easiest path is heading directly into it, because the wind has an equal effect on the boat. and the stern paddler can control the boat easily. But let's say the direct route to your destination means the wind is coming at you from the side. If you aim directly for your target, the wind is going to push you off-course, and the stern paddler has to correct the direction constantly. Instead, point the canoe away from the target, more into the wind, and continue to paddle forward, as shown for Boat 2 in the illustration on page 105. The stern paddler will need to do fewer corrective strokes, and the wind will slip the boat sideways nicely and push you toward your destination. This move is called a *ferry* because it's just like a river ferry moving from one side of the river to the other.

A FAMILY AFFAIR

Canoeing with kids is great when their needs are recognized. Ignore a child's desire to stop, explore, swim, and hike, and you're guaranteed to have a grueling tour. My family has always treated the canoe like a playroom or playground. Favorite toys are accessible in the boat rather than packed away, and towing kids who swim along off the stern line is considered a cool thing by kids and adults. It's a good workout for the canoeists, too, as the kids get older! Barbie has her own duct-taped canoe and negotiates the "rapids" of feeder brooks with considerable skill at the hands of a six-year-old, and waterfalls in the brook are within our Barbie's range of canoeing skills. These priorities are helpful:

- Fun!

- More fun!

- Stop before it stops being fun!

Remember that a four- to five-mile flatwater canoe tour might be just fine for you, but it can be an eternity to a bored child. The pre-toddler months are nice and relatively easy because babies often sleep through the experience, lulled by the roll of the canoe. For the toddler stage, my brother-in-law built a crib-style railing in the center of his canoe so his kids could stand up without toppling over the side. It allowed the kids to move when they got antsy and eliminated the need for restraint by par-

Treat a canoe like a playground for your kids.

ents, who were able to paddle with fewer interruptions.

Once a child wants to grasp a paddle, put one in her hands for as little or as long as she wants. Kid-sized models with short shafts are available from some manufacturers. By elementary school, children want to sit on a seat and paddle, although usually in a spurt-and-die fashion. It's helpful to know how to paddle the canoe solo because that's essentially what you will be doing. I once watched a father-daughter team race down a whitewater-canoe slalom course, sliding between the slalom poles with almost no touches. The father was clearly a skilled paddler and racer, but his six-year-old daughter knew her bow strokes and executed them strongly. What a wonderful team to watch! Good technical skills can be learned at an early age, if children are interested, and they may be less fearful of swimming rapids than you are. Attitude is a key factor. In that same slalom race, I watched a father-and-son team paddle the same course; the father yelled at the 13-year-old son, who ended up crying in their car and refusing to paddle a second time. The judges wanted to award penalty points to the father for emotional abuse of a young canoeist.

Young children can paddle exceedingly well with the right introduction and even some unorthodox but effective strategies. At her father's encouragement, Becky Mason began to solo paddle in an 11-foot birchbark canoe at seven years old: "I was thrilled with the idea, but my one worry I expressed was not being able to return to the safety of the dock. So to solve my worries of not getting back, Dad got a hundred-foot length of yellow floating rope, attached one end to the dock and the other end to the stern. I had a really great time that summer, reveling in my 100 feet of freedom, happy in the knowledge that I was secure. Even if a choppy wind lifted me up and tried to take me away, I'd always feel the reassuring tug of the line when I reached the end. My big moment in canoeing that I

INTERNATIONAL SCALE OF RIVER DIFFICULTY

• • • • • • • • • • • • • • • • •

(continued from page 106)

boat control in tight passages or around ledges often required. Strong eddies and powerful currents found. Scouting advisable for inexperienced parties. Group-assisted rescues may be necessary to avoid long swims.

- **Class IV: Advanced.** Intense, powerful, predictable rapids requiring precise boat-handling in turbulent water. Large, unavoidable waves, holes, and constricted passages require fast moves under pressure. A fast, reliable eddy turn may be necessary to stop, scout, or rest. Risk of injury to swimmers is moderate to high, and water conditions may make self-rescue difficult.

- **Class V: Expert** and **Class VI: Extreme.** Usually apply to kayakers.

• •

"Canoeing together has created strong family ties—as any shared experience will do."

— Marge Shepardson, age 51

• •

remember so well was when I decided that I didn't need the safety of my tether. I untied the line and set off on my little solo adventures in my beloved birchbark canoe."

Sometimes the packing up of young children and canoe gear can take longer than the actual experience itself, unless you choose a stretch that allows exploration on land and breaks up the time spent confined in the canoe. That remains true for older children as well. By junior high, mixing canoeing with other attractions can be important to maintain interest. I've camped on islands with fast-moving current and no obstacles in the river channels, where the kids spent hours floating in their life jackets from the top of the island, swimming back in to catch the bottom eddy, and hiking back up the cobble beach to the top. Not only is it great fun, it's also great self-rescue practice.

Marge Shepardson began canoeing at four years old and followed that tradition with her own family: "Carl and I continued to canoe after our children were born; we just bought a bigger canoe and brought them with us. Eventually, canoe-tripping became not so much a vacation as a way of life—when summer came, you went canoeing (sometimes for the whole summer). Although kids can be just as fussy on canoe trips as they are at home, I like to think that ours have benefitted in unique ways from these trips. They have experienced different cultures from traveling though the north, they have learned to be confident and self-reliant, and they have certainly learned to tolerate discomfort! When something's not going well at home, they can always say, 'It could be worse!' Finally, it has created strong family ties—as any shared experience will do." The Shepardsons tell stories about their many experiences on North American rivers in *The Family Canoe Trip: A Unique Approach to Family Canoeing* (see listing in chapter 11).

SAFE TRAVEL TIPS ON THE WATER

Managing your canoe trip safely is your responsibility, and you must be aware of the guidelines for safe travel that are recognized by the canoeing community. The advice here is based on the American Whitewater Safety Code, which is designed to improve canoeing and kayaking safety in the sport. You also must be aware of your state's specific regulations for boating that may affect what you can do. For example, some states require that a life jacket actually be worn during cold weather rather than just be available in the canoe. In Massachusetts, we have to wear a life jacket between October 15 and May 15.

These general safety guidelines can help:

- Avoid drugs because they impair judgment

- Paddle with a support group

- Establish a clear organization

- Understand your responsibilities to the group

- Use a signal system to communicate

- Have a schedule and keep to it

Don't consume alcohol or other drugs while boating. A disturbing factor in canoeing accidents is impaired judgment from drug consumption, whether it's flatwater or whitewater accidents. Flatwater canoeists with impaired balance can easily tip the boat; whitewater paddlers with impaired decision-making abilities cannot read rapids as well and negotiate the route. Save the celebration for the end of the day. Be rested, well fed, and well hydrated to canoe safely—the safety of others in your group may depend on it.

Boating alone is discouraged because no one will be able to provide assistance if you need it. A party of three canoes offers better security because two rescue boats are more stable than one in the catamaran-style T rescue discussed in chapter 7. If you boat alone, the best locations are small, protected bodies of water near the shoreline, where you can swim easily to shore to get out of cold water.

Every group—but especially solo canoeists—should leave a float plan with family or friends. The plan identifies your access points, itinerary and, most importantly, your expected return time. Your contact will know where any search should begin if you are excessively late.

A group needs to establish organizational rules to keep the party intact. Small groups may decide to stay within voice or visual contact and can paddle easily without a strict organization. But larger groups can get separated easily over longer distances, and they function best with clearly designated roles. The *lead* boat sets a comfortable pace that doesn't demoralize the least-skilled canoeists. The lead paddlers should be good map- or river-readers who can choose the route, and they can carry rescue throw bags to set up a safety system at harder rapids when paddling whitewater. A *sweep*, or last, boat makes sure that all other canoes are ahead of it to keep the group together. The last boat also should have first-aid supplies, rescue gear, and extra gear such as paddles. The canoeists should be skilled in rescue and first-aid techniques and able to paddle quickly downriver in the event of an emergency.

With large differences in ability, some groups divide into "faster" and "slower" groups that agree to meet up at a prearranged point—usually a location that offers the early group an interesting diversion. Another strategy is to equalize abilities between canoes so that a lesser-skilled paddler is paired with a more highly skilled paddler. One of the challenges of tandem paddling is dealing with these differences. I find that voice contact between canoeists encourages sociability and emotional comfort; relying primarily on visual contact enhances solitude. The mood of a group determines what is best, and it may vary daily depending on environmental conditions. The more difficult the conditions, the closer the physical organization of canoes—although sufficient spacing is necessary to avoid collisions. Canoeists may travel 50 feet apart in easier rapids but then expand the distance to 150 feet in intricate rapids, where you may need to paddle around another canoe stuck on a rock.

Canoeists in the middle of the pack have responsibilities for the group's overall organization. Especially on wilderness trips, we ask canoeists to keep track of the boat ahead and—most importantly—the boat behind them. If the following canoe stops or slows down, then you should, too, until they catch up. A ripple effect should occur to the front of the group until the lead boat has slowed or stopped. A boat that fails to heed this principle may be responsible for a breakdown in organization that can result in an unnerving lack of communication, lost canoes, and an inability of the group to respond to a potential problem.

Each canoe also has a responsibility to communicate messages to the preceding and following boat in the lineup. Knowing the American Whitewater Affiliation's river signal system is helpful for routine route choices and emergency situations. The "stop" signal means a potential hazard may be ahead; canoeists should hold position in the river by back-paddling or going to shore as soon as they can safely do so (see illustration at bottom, this page). Before continuing downriver, they scout the situation or wait for the "all clear" signal (illustration page 111, top left). The "emergency-stop" signal, which also could be three long blasts on a whistle, means that a life-threatening situation is unfolding downriver. The signaling canoeist will signal the designated rescue canoe to respond to the emergency; all other canoeists should hold position in the river, assess the situation, and respond to the emergency as necessary (illustration page 111, top right). For paddlers inexperienced in rescue, the best response simply may be paddling to shore and awaiting further direction. After scouting, you also can signal the correct route by tipping your paddle to the side of the river that you want others to descend.

Finally, it is wise to establish a schedule and stick to it. Know what your turnaround time should be on a loop or out-and-back trip, realizing

Above: Adequate spacing in whitewater helps you to avoid collisions. **Right:** Signal "stop" by holding your paddle with both hands over your head, gripping it along the shaft and keeping the paddle parallel to the water surface. Flexing your arms to move the paddle up and down usually indicates an urgent need to stop quickly.

Stop

that people may be more fatigued for the return trip and paddle slower. Plan for bad-weather days on trips (at least one day per week) and have a miles-per-day projection. I've been on wilderness trips where we have to average 15 miles daily to reach our ending point in time to make a rendezvous with chartered planes. On a two-month journey in northern Canada, we actually paddle more than 15 miles a day at the beginning to get ahead a little. Regions with big lakes and a history of storms require that kind of conservative approach, and knowing you're ahead of schedule takes the edge off of being winded for four days. I'm less twitchy in my storm-battered tent when I know I have a margin of extra time to make up those lost days.

Signal "**all clear**" by holding your paddle in front of you with the blade straight up in the air; slide one hand up the shaft to stabilize the paddle. Signal "**emergency stop**" by waving an object over your head; with the other hand, you can give three long blasts on your whistle.

All clear

Emergency stop

UNDERSTANDING WHITEWATER RIVERS

The character of a river is a function of the underlying geology; how the water flows over rocks, gravel, and sand determines how exciting your journey will be. Look not only at the bouncing water, but also at the surrounding terrain for clues about what makes the water meander or jump. Understanding a river's colorful features is necessary in picking a good route. With experience, you'll be able to see the lines of current that create nice channels between rocks and ledges. Distinct features will emerge from water that Jean McIntyre of New Hampshire describes as "frothy as a vanilla milkshake."

Deborah Laun, 37, an industrial designer from Syracuse, New York, describes the reward of learning to understand a river: "People wonder why I call myself a wimp when I kayak Class IV, run a waterfall or two, and canoe in the rain and bugs for three weeks and call it a honeymoon (George River, 1992). The reason is that I don't push myself to the limit of my abilities (being a mom). It took me at least three years to learn to Eskimo roll. It's this fear thing. It took me a long time to get any good, and I hardly ever dump because of playing it safe. This cowardice led to amazing river-reading skills. I think of it as a second language. . . . My biggest thrill on whitewater is being faced with a confusion of white and in seconds sorting out a route, adjusting, using the water to maneuver, with a well-timed stroke, a lean, a rudder; to ferry across a river with just two paddle strokes, surfing, ruddering. It is art, not power."

Water can be a powerful force, and whitewater rivers deserve respect. Never stand up in current in a river unless the water is barely above your ankles. Once your feet are planted on the river bottom, the current still wants to push against your legs and push you over. If your feet get trapped, you could get pushed underwater. Remember the self-rescue position described in chapter 7, swim to shore, and don't stand up until your buttocks bump on the rocks in shallow water.

River bends

As water slips lazily downhill in its search for the path of least resistance, inertia forces it to flow to the outside of a curve. The fastest, deepest water will be on the outside of a river bend. In shallower streams, you probably want to follow this deep channel. However, be aware of the surrounding soil and vegetation. The water can erode a soft, sandy outer bank, and you need to watch for trees whose root systems have been undercut. When these trees topple into the river, they become *strainers*, where water flows through submerged branches. Paddle away from them immediately or, if floating toward one, be prepared to swim up on top of the tree or log. On big, bouncing rivers when you can't see around the bend, you may want to avoid the outside channel and stay tight to the inside of the bend. The water is shallower and slower here and, although not as exciting, it does allow you to scout what is around the corner.

fast, deep outside bends

slow, shallow inside bends

Deeper channels are found on the outside of river bends. The inside bends often have shallow shoals (rock or sand beds).

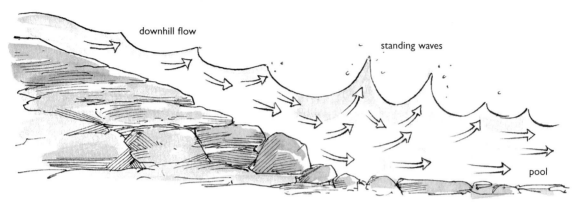

downhill flow

standing waves

pool

Waves build as fast water crashes into water moving more slowly.

River width

As water flows downhill within the riverbed, it reacts to a constriction or expansion of river width. As the river banks come closer together, the water flows through a narrower slot and the constriction forces some of the water upward into the air. Waves form as lines of current slam together in the middle of the channel. The effect is heightened if the river flattens and widens slightly into a *pool* just below. The fast waves hit the slow-moving, deeper pool and bounce even higher as the energy, needing to go somewhere, bounces into the air. If the river widens but continues to drop in elevation, then it gets shallower and runs quickly around obstacles, forming *rapids*.

Downstream Vs

A constriction can occur between two rocks in the river. When water hits an obstacle such as a rock, it veers off in an angular direction. These lines of current between rocks can create a channel similar to the constriction described previously, although they may be subtler in gentler water. They form a **V** shape, with the bottom of the **V** pointing downstream. This point is often where you want to direct the canoe to miss the obstacles that cause the **V**.

Eddies

As water hits a rock, it separates and swirls around behind the obstruction to fill in the area on the downstream side known as an *eddy*. The current actually flows back upstream behind the rock, hits the rock again, and swirls back into the main current. Eddies are a great place to stop, rest, and decide the next move because their upstream-flowing current helps keep your canoe behind the obstruction. An *eddy line* is created between the main current (heading downstream) and the recirculating eddy current (heading upstream), often spotted because the friction from these opposing currents causes swirls or boils.

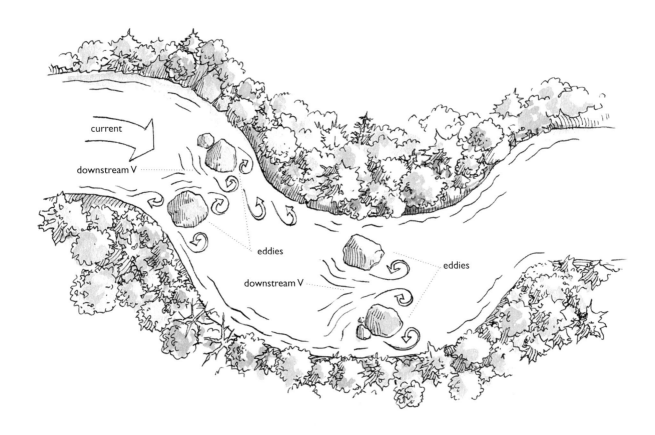

Because eddy lines can be unstable, you want to cross them decisively before turning the canoe into the eddy. Turning strokes are best executed in the eddy water, which offers good support for your paddle—not on a boiling and unstable eddy line that will suck the blade to the river bottom!

Pillows and holes

When a small layer of water flows over a rock or ledge, it flows in a smoother sheen that is slightly elevated from the main current. It looks like a slightly puffed *pillow*. Pillows are hard to spot because the water is only subtly disturbed, and you often see them when your bow slides up on them. Then your canoe is *broached* on the rock. Wiggle off it or let your boat spin in the current, always leaning downstream to prevent the canoe's upstream side from being pushed underwater by the current. The speed of the spinning often pulls the canoe off the rock; a little hip-shimmy can help inch it off as well. If these methods fail, prepare to step out of the canoe on its downstream side, onto the rock or into a shallow eddy. The boat will lift easily once your weight leaves the boat; you then can pivot it into the eddy and hop back in.

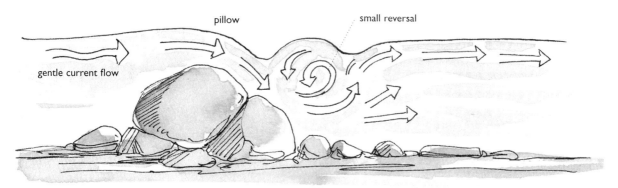

Shallow water can mound over rocks and look like a **pillow**.

As river volume increases, more water will flow over the top of the obstacles. The bigger the obstacle, the bigger the depression below it that will fill up with water. If the hole below the rock is big, then water will drop sharply over the rock, hit the river bottom, and curl back on itself. This tight curl of water below the rock is known as a *hole* or *reversal* because the eddy water is flowing forcefully back upstream to fill in the depression. The length of a hole behind the obstruction is believed to be equal to its depth. With experience, a hole that is several feet long can be fun to play in by surfing it, but avoid the bigger ones known as *keepers* because they'll keep your boat and you recirculating in the hole.

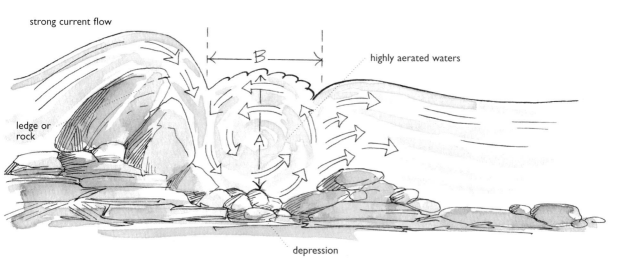

The river will churn in the depression below an obstacle and form a **hole**.

ROUTE-FINDING IN WHITEWATER

Let's talk about role responsibilities for a moment because route-finding can create problems for tandem canoeists. I advocate putting your fastest thinker in the bow because she can make quick decisions about the best route after reading the river terrain. With a quick gesture of the paddle, she can communicate the route and begin pulling her bow that way. The stern paddler has the responsibility to get her stern end into the same channel, "reading" the body language of the bow canoeist, as well as the river features, to do it. And she has the extra two seconds she may need to process the scene. I explained this strategy in a *Canoe & Kayak* article in 1996 when I was a technique editor; later that year, two women in an advanced semiprivate lesson told me it saved their partnership. Forget the old notion of putting the best paddler or river reader in the stern to "captain" the canoe; put her in the bow where she can communicate *visually* as well as verbally—it's usually what the other paddler needs.

Two different strategies in river-running exist: conservative and playful. The conservative approach is usually adopted by canoeists with gear packed into the canoe; the playful approach is often desired by daytrippers looking for excitement. The conservative approach puts a premium on staying dry and avoiding capsizing so you don't have the dubious pleasure of rescuing your food, clothing, shelter, and transportation! The playful approach encourages the use of more aggressive and complex maneuvers amid challenging obstacles.

The conservative approach

Conservative paddling requires a strong back stroke to slow the canoe. You often travel at the same speed as or slower than the current. Back-paddling gives canoeists more time to scout the best route and make decisions. It's also useful in standing waves to stay dry—the boat rides up over waves rather than crashing through them.

Canoe-trippers can seek the slower water to the inside of river bends, which will keep them out of bouncing waves near the outside shore. They use the *back* or *downstream ferry*, where they keep their upstream (stern) end angled toward the slower shore and back-paddle around the corner. Back-paddling prevents the canoe from slipping into the faster water and it slides the canoe into the eddy just below the corner. The current will help push the canoe there if the boat is moving at or slower than the current speed. The crucial part is keeping the upstream end angled enough toward shore so that it slips over the eddy line decisively and before the bow. Usually, both paddlers need to execute quick turning strokes to keep the upstream end angled into the eddy, and then immediately resume back strokes to continue slowing the canoe. It's a slick move!

Playing the river

Canoeists can deliberately choose the most exciting channels, waves, and eddies to play the river. They use a forward stroke to charge aggressively across current, usually traveling faster than the

Conservative route-finding, where a **back ferry** allows you to scout the route.

current speed. The canoes are filled with flotation because this riskier approach can result in more frequent capsizing and rescues. However, riding the edge between disaster and success is the challenge! A playful approach allows me to combine a series of thrilling maneuvers in a flowing sequence, and I strive to create smoothly my own river dance in more and more difficult whitewater.

One of the most common maneuvers is the *upstream* or *forward ferry,* which allows the boat to move quickly across current. The principles are the same as the back ferry, only now the canoe faces upstream and paddlers use forward strokes to maintain position in the river. Point your upstream end (bow) toward the opposite shore as an angle against the main current, which will begin to push you toward your destination. Play with the degree of boat angle against the current to see its effect. The more upstream the bow is pointed, the slower you'll move across the river because less canoe is exposed to oncoming current. Expose more of the canoe side by pointing the bow more toward the desired shore, then watch how fast the canoe moves across the river. The stern paddler in the downstream end will find it easier to maintain the boat angle against the current; the bow paddler in the upstream end usually just paddles hard forward with assistance from the stern.

Other useful maneuvers are the U-turns described in chapter 6. They allow you to turn in to and out of the eddies, where the current helps to spin the canoe. However, you have to remember an important variable when performing U-turns in the river: Lean the boat into the turns to

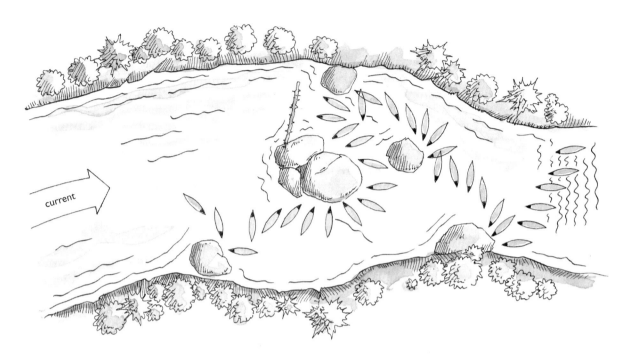

Aggressive play encourages the use of eddy turns, peelouts, and upstream ferries to dart in and out of eddies.

counteract the river's desire to flip the canoe over. If you don't lean enough, the current will try to grab the outside edge of the canoe and force it underwater. You are actually leaning downstream into the current you are entering.

A U-turn when entering an eddy is called an *eddy turn*, where you end up facing upstream in the security of the eddy—a nice resting spot from which to scout the next move. A U-turn that lets you leave the eddy and continue forward downriver is called a *peelout* because the downstream current catches the bow and quickly spins the canoe around. Most swims happen here, when canoeists fail to lean hard into the turn and the main current strikes the upstream side of the canoe, sucking the gunwale down. You roll upstream into the river—and get to practice the whitewater rescue skills introduced in chapter 7.

TRIP ESSENTIALS

Beyond technical considerations for canoe trips, women need to examine some other important factors. Treasured gear is a key area—the stuff you learn to take on every trip after the first one, when you discover you desperately want the forgotten item. My husband calls it "fine-tuning the rig." Even after decades of canoe trips, I am still adjusting my list of important items. Canoeing is a sensory experience, and enticing food is a big deal on many trips. No day is a canned-stew day! Women's opinions about canoe-trip essentials are plentiful and lively.

Gear I wouldn't travel without

- My Pendleton wool shirt

- My ax, which my Dad gave me to take to camp in the seventh grade. I still have the original handle on it

- My sense of humor and adventure. Without it, I would have succumbed to the elements

- Rubber boots. The boots are invaluable in the north because you can load the boat, fill the water bottles, walk through mud or wet grass, and still stay dry. They also protect your ankles from bugs

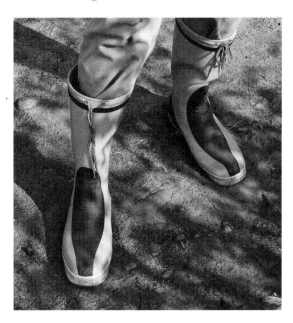

Gear you wouldn't leave at home.

- My journal . . . it gives me a place to work out ideas and a place to draw on rest days

- Crazy Creek chair

- Gel seat and Crazy Creek chair combined

- Kneepads for old knees

- A dry bag nearby for extras like warm clothes and snacks

- Two pairs of ski poles with handles and baskets removed: the tips are inserted into hollow ends to make long poles that lie on the bottom of the canoe to keep packs off the bottom; the poles serve as tarp poles and can be put back together as ski poles for fording streams

- My river sandals—no more wet wool socks and squishy tennis shoes!

- Box for day gear—I use a watertight ammunition box

- Bent-shaft paddle—it feels good in my hand, and it just fits me nicely

- A big insulated coffee mug retrofitted with a plunger for making coffee

- 25 rolls of film for a month-long trip

- A blow-up pillow—forget rolling up a jacket

- A plastic jug filled with water for ballast when it's really windy

- Rescue knife attached to my life jacket

- Bailer—dual function—gets the water out of the canoe and saves having to leave the tent in the middle of the night when the bugs are fierce or it's raining

- My Advil!

Trip food that makes your mouth water

- Pizza bread cooked in a reflector or Dutch oven

- Fresh blueberries or raspberries growing along the river

- Special brownies from the outback oven with chocolate pudding sort of melted on top

- Best meal in my whole life: Arctic char on the George River cooked in butter on a tin stove in an Inuit canvas tent

- Fruitcake soaked in rum

- Dried melon—like candy!

- Brown bears in the apple orchard—an old Girl Scout dessert—with applesauce in the bottom of the pan and the gingerbread mix with only half the liquid globbed on top; the applesauce steams the gingerbread

- My husband's homemade donuts

- Bacon—after reading Hemingway's Nick Adams stories on a two-month Arctic trip, in which he describes bacon in painstaking, sizzling detail and all I had was granola

- Hot chocolate with peppermint schnapps

- Blueberry-pecan pancakes my sons and I made together

- Mashed-potato stew with dried potatoes, onions, fried Hickory Farms beefstick, and melted Monterey Jack cheese

- Strawberry shortcake in a Dutch oven

- Fresh hot bread

- Cheese fondue for two in front of our Baker tent perched by a waterfall far away from civilization—a menu item and a restaurant that I'd paddle anywhere for

- My favorite is to catch walleye, fillet it, coat it with a special batter, and cook it over an open wood fire—it's so fresh you can taste the wiggle!

Chapter 10

TIPS AND MORE TIPS

CONDITIONING FOR CANOEING

Once you've gotten hooked on canoeing, you will find that improved conditioning will allow longer tours and more vigorous paddling. You'll feel more energetic and less fatigue in handling a paddle. Now, I'm not advocating extensive sessions at the fitness center for everyone—weight-lifting and stationary exercise machines make me yawn,

Stretch gently in the canoe to warm up for paddling.

and the scenery never changes! But they do have great value for canoeing, which is largely an upper-body activity. Rowing machines are especially effective in targeting canoeing muscles such as the abdomen, and cross-country-ski simulators work the torso and arms well. Staff can help you develop a light lifting program that focuses on the arms, chest, abdomen, and back.

I like to develop general canoeing fitness by participating regularly in a variety of activities. I've found that regular cross-country skiing and swimming can strengthen paddling muscles and keep me outdoors in fresh air, which is most important to me. Bicycling, walking, and jogging are excellent to improve overall cardiorespiratory fitness and increase stamina, but they do little for upper-body conditioning. However, they allow me to vary my fitness activities and stay interested in working out on a regular basis.

If you are waking up dormant parts of your body, stretching is an excellent way to prevent injury and relieve muscle soreness! I advocate stretching lightly after you have warmed up with some gentle paddling, and then stretching more completely at the end of your canoeing experience. Stretching also increases your flexibility, which can be useful in more efficiently executing some strokes. Your ability to reach across the bow is really enhanced. I discovered that my torso wasn't really flexible, but I've made good improvements in this area with these stretches. Remember to breathe evenly and deeply throughout each one, and stretch slowly to the point of tension. At no point should you experience any pain. Begin with larger muscles before smaller ones, and hold each stretch for 15 seconds.

In-the-boat stretching

While sitting or kneeling in the canoe, stretch out your arms like a turnstile, rotate your torso, and try to line up your arms with the centerline of the canoe. Stretch until you feel resistance in your torso muscles. Note how close you can get to this parallel alignment and use it as a future reference. Repeat by swiveling your torso in the other direction. Do you have increased or decreased flexibility in this direction, compared to the other side? Repeat the stretch on both sides, trying to rotate your arms a little past your previous mark.

Now stretch the torso with an overhead reach. Interlace your figures above your head with palms facing up. Reach upward toward the sky with your hands. You should feel a stretch in the arms, shoulders, and upper back.

Focus on the shoulders with an elbow pull. Raise one arm above your head, then bend it so your hand is behind your back, between the shoulders. With your other hand, grasp your elbow and pull down and back. Gradually apply more pressure to increase the stretch. Continue on the other side.

Finish with wrist circles. Rotate your wrists so your hands form circles in the air. Extend your fingers to keep your hands relaxed. Repeat in the other direction.

Stretching after canoeing

Repeat the torso twists. If you want to stretch on land, spread your feet shoulder-width and place a paddle between your feet. Swivel your torso to line up your arms with the paddle. Now try a variation on the torso twist. With a paddle resting on your shoulders, bend forward at the waist. Twist your torso until one hand points toward the opposite foot.

Elbow pull.

Hip-torso stretch.

Now lean straight forward from the waist without locking your legs or twisting the torso. Let your arms dangle limply and your head drop forward, which should relax any tension in the neck and shoulders. Hold for 30 seconds, then lift the torso slowly, letting your head rise last.

Repeat the overhead reach to the sky. Then tilt your stretched arms to one side, holding the position before you come upright, then tilt your arms to the other side. You should feel the stretch in your shoulder and side.

Because your hips may feel tight from sitting on the seat, a hip-torso stretch can be useful. Stretch one leg in front of you, then cross the other leg over it at the knee. Twist your torso away from the outstretched leg. Use your arm to press against the knee. Repeat on the other side.

Repeat the elbow pull and wrist circles.

PADDLING WHILE PREGNANT

Canoeing is an excellent way to feel relatively weightless during pregnancy—the boat bears your weight rather than your hip, leg, and ankle joints. As your body is changing its shape and center of balance, you can achieve a measure of graceful gliding in a canoe that is impossible on land! Canoeing offers non-jarring exercise throughout a pregnancy and can be a rewarding way to stay active, even during the last trimester. While there are physical benefits to remaining active during pregnancy, more women comment on how important canoeing is psychologically by offering freedom of movement and a means to travel easily.

Check with your healthcare provider to determine the level of intensity that might be appropriate for you and your baby and the duration of the activity during your pregnancy. Some women paddle nearly to the day of delivery because they can paddle more comfortably than they can walk. However, be aware of how the changes in your body affect your stance and stamina in the canoe.

As your center of gravity moves forward and higher, it can change how you are balanced in the canoe. A smaller range of motion in your torso will have a greater impact in tipping the canoe, so you'll want to be conservative in leaning into strokes until you gain a sense of your new balance. You may find that kneeling in the canoe makes you feel more secure than sitting on the seat; however, it may not be a good option if you have tender knees.

Canoeing can give you freedom of movement when pregnant.

While you can still rotate your torso through your strokes in the early stages, women usually find that by the third trimester they cannot swivel their upper bodies as much or at all. The forward stroke becomes more dependent on your arms, which can be more quickly fatiguing. Adjust your trip distances accordingly or plan breaks into the schedule so you have time to rest during a tour.

Executing turning strokes can be more difficult because you can't twist your body as easily to each side. (Cross strokes are often impossible because you can't reach across your belly.) You may have to give up playing in whitewater rapids and enjoy straight downriver runs. Skilled paddlers who continue to paddle whitewater stretches usually adopt more conservative river-running strategies because they don't want to capsize and get jounced into obstacles in the rapids. They heed more closely the one question that all canoeists should ask themselves in determining whether to run a rapid: Am I willing to swim it?

Suzanne Tromara, 40, a technical writer from Buckland, Massachusetts, remembers canoeing a Class II whitewater stretch of the Farmington River in Connecticut when she was six months pregnant: "The rapid looked a lot bigger to me than it ever had. I felt a lot less confident because I couldn't paddle the same way. And there was no way I was going to swim, because it was October."

Suzanne, a long-time canoeist and kayaker, couldn't fit into her regular paddling gear any longer, so she was wearing her husband's oversized clothing, which felt strange. She had spent most of her pregnancy fighting a lot of nausea and vomiting, and, inactive all summer as a result, she felt physically weaker. But, as that phase passed, Suzanne embraced canoeing again. "I felt so alive and so happy because I could finally do something. It was wonderful. I had a great time, " she said.

Low-back pain is a common complaint during pregnancy, so you'll want to stretch more frequently. A foam pad on the seat helps relieve stress, and traveling closer to shore is important for getting out to stretch. This strategy allows the added benefit of more frequent stops for an active bladder!

"Bathroom" breaks become more frequent, especially since the sound of moving water seems to encourage an urge to urinate. Bea von Hagke, 36, a community development specialist from Deerfield, Massachusetts, paddled the Snake River in Wyoming while five months pregnant. "It felt like I needed to stop every 15 minutes," she said. "Pregnancy makes you dehydrated, so you drink more water and then you have to stop more." Bea and her husband Dan were amused by his sympathetic response—he found that he had the urge to go every time she did. Count on canoeing fewer miles than before!

Hot, humid weather can be a problem during pregnancy because your body may be more sensitive to the heat. Remember that you'll be heated by the sun in two ways when paddling: directly from above and from the reflected glare off the water. Drink plenty of water to stay hydrated, wear a brimmed hat and sunscreen for sun protection, and swim or float frequently to cool down.

Some women experience a problem with queasiness early in their pregnancy, particularly when the wind kicks up waves, but other women have no problems at all. Some women become incredibly sleepy when paddling; amused partners can simply paddle solo during these catnaps. By the last trimester, a life jacket may fit poorly around your middle and have a tendency to ride up; however, some manufacturers produce models with leg straps that you can attach and adjust to your new size (discussed in chapter 8). The straps will keep the life jacket more securely on your body when you float in it.

Let your body be your guide: Stop any activity that makes you feel uncomfortable. Consult your healthcare provider if you are planning an extended trip where medical services may not be readily available. Many women say the canoe-camping trips during pregnancy have been especially meaningful with their partners—and they set the stage nicely for being mobile by canoe with the new addition.

CANOEING WITH A PHYSICAL LIMITATION

Paddling can provide marvelous mobility for people with physical limitations, particularly lower-body impairments. It may be the key to freedom for some who have difficulty walking, and essential to a feeling of independence for those who have to rely on others to be mobile. Once appropriate equipment adaptations are devised, the canoeing experience is essentially the same for all paddlers, regardless of ability.

Annie Wortham Webre and Janet Zeller write in the American Canoe Association's *Canoeing and Kayaking Instruction Manual for Persons with Physical Disabilities* that "Paddling is a sport which emphasizes ability. Skill is determined by ability and attitude, whether the paddler is able-bodied or disabled. . . . The freedom paddling offers pushes aside the barriers presented by disabilities. A body which may be uncooperative on land becomes part of a sleek craft gliding through the water. Together paddlers, able-bodied and disabled, can share all aspects of the sport. Water is the ultimate equalizer."

Janet, the ACA president, knows first-hand how important paddling can be to people with physical limitations. Reflex dystrophy has forced her into a wheelchair, and, in the manual, she writes movingly of the role paddling plays in her life: "The freedom I discover each time I paddle is a gift to my spirit."

I once led a two-day canoe trip for older women; Lois Harris, an 80-ish contributor to the section on aging in the book *Our Bodies, Our Selves*, worried whether she should participate. A hip problem prevented her from walking easily, especially on uneven ground, but we assured her that the group could help her with camp chores and getting in and out of a canoe. Lois had

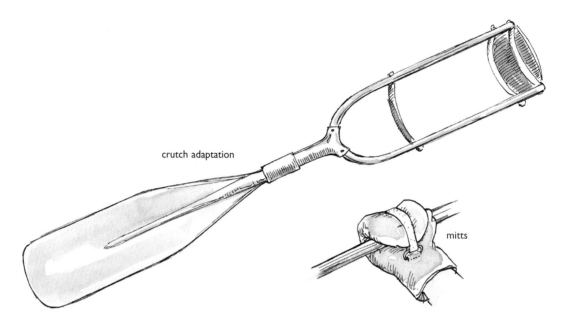

crutch adaptation

mitts

Simple adaptations will let you grasp the paddle.

learned to paddle as a Girl Scout 70 years earlier; with a quick review, her J stroke was as efficient as ever in the stern. Good thing, too, because her hip injury allowed her to paddle on one side only. However, fatigue didn't appear to be a problem—she and her partner talked endlessly and canoed ahead of the pack both days. That's what good technique can do!

Adaptations of canoes and paddles allow people with limitations to paddle quite well. Mitts attached to a paddle or crutches blended with paddles help those without clasping ability; canoe seats with upright structural support stabilize a person with limited or no trunk balance. People with visual impairments can canoe whitewater if they have a strong verbal communication system with their partner. Paddlers with a hearing loss can develop visual hand signals to communicate about whitewater features in difficult sections.

The American Canoe Association developed a great training program for its instructors, and its helpful *Canoeing and Kayaking Instructional Manual for Persons with Physical Disabilities*, provides you with tools to develop adaptations (see the listing in chapter 11). If you have a physical limitation, begin with professional instruction so that your introduction is a sound and safe one. The ACA also can tell you which instructors in your area have been trained by its Disabled Paddlers Committee.

CANOEING RESPONSIBLY

As more people use waterways for recreation, our lakes and rivers show the impact. Trash, noise, vehicular wakes, campfires, and erosion take their toll on the lake and river landscapes. Canoeists have a responsibility to adopt a minimum-impact approach to waterway use so that we preserve and respect the natural resources that enable us to enjoy the outdoors. Consider that activity on lake and river shores is usually restricted to within several hundred feet of the water— less in regions with dense underbrush—which means that impact is concentrated in a very narrow area along the shore. Adopt this guiding principle for canoe travel: Leave your route cleaner and better looking than you found it.

I teach in the Outdoor Leadership Program at Greenfield Community College in Massachusetts. My students once collected six bags of garbage from an Adirondacks campsite frequented by powerboaters. You may be picking up the refuse left by other users, but you are leaving the best record of your own use: no record at all. Develop a pack-it-out trash ethic, including toilet paper and food leftovers. Some people like to burn used toilet paper at the site, but do so only if you can burn it completely—but not at all in dry conditions. Burying leftover food doesn't prevent animals from digging it up, so plan your meals carefully. Otherwise, you should pack it out—a colossal chore that I try to avoid by cooking careful amounts.

Other aspects of traveling responsibly need to be considered:

- Personal and group hygiene

- Cooking- and tent-site management

- Established "rules of the road"

- Wildlife watching

The environment can determine which protocols are best—a desert trip is very different from a northern-woods experience. Check locally to find out the preferred guidelines for responsible travel, which may have changed since your last visit due to the pressures of increased visitors in the area. For instance, the recommendation for personal hygiene on Maine's fragile coastal islands used to be that all hygiene happened below tideline. Now, paddlers are asked to create their own portable latrines, which can be as simple as lining a plastic bucket or ammunition box with a plastic bag filled with kitty litter. The unit comes home with you for disposal in your landfill rather than the dumpster at the local marina.

In general, all washing happens 200 feet from a water source to allow adequate filtration back into the water table. I minimize my use of soap on trips, reserving it only for limited personal washing. Dishes can be washed well with hot water and sand, dirt, leaves, or pine needles as scouring agents. Really!

Before trampling vegetation to create a new site, use established cooking and tent sites where the soil is already quite hard. Stay on existing trails leading up from the water's edge so you don't create new erosion paths. River shoes without heavy tread work well to minimize impact. When setting up a new site, choose cooking and tent sites away from shore on durable surfaces such as ledge and sand. Leave the aesthetic sites overlooking the water for community use, which is likely to be lighter than repeated trips to cooking/sleeping sites.

You can get quite close to wildlife with a quiet stroke.

The campfire issue is a thorny one for people who associate outdoor travel with the romance of a fire. I usually make fires only in established fire pits where "dead and down" brush and limbs are available. Never cut live boughs—they burn poorly and create scars or "hatchet lines" above the head (as high as a person with an ax can reach). The only place in recent memory that I cooked with wood was on a three-week canoe trip in northern Norway, where the forest is thick with downed trees and the gravel bars provide good cooking sites. Otherwise, I always cook on camp stoves and try to wean kids off the idea that a fire is a necessity every night.

Know the "rules of the road" on rivers with lots of traffic, and paddle defensively. Usually staying to the right is the best approach. Keep tight to shore when traveling amid motorized boat traffic because a canoe is small enough so as to be hard to see. Tighten up your group organization so other boaters don't have to weave through your party. Polite boaters will slow down to reduce the impact of their wake. At night I have a light in the boat so I can make myself visible to other traffic, if necessary. Polite canoeists will give anglers lots of room.

Observing wildlife is one of the reasons I canoe, but you can have an adverse impact if you intrude too closely. Be careful of nesting birds and denning animals, because disturbing them may have a negative impact on the next generation. We avoid the known nesting spots for loons on a southern New Hampshire lake where we have a summer camp, giving the mothers and their young a wide berth when they're first afloat.

Consider these strategies to watch the Big One, and if you're successful, you may end up closer than you thought possible.

- Paddle quietly without talking as you approach.

- Approach an animal head-on so less of the canoe is visible.

- Avoid flashing your wet blade, which will reflect sun and spook animals; feather the blade low to the water or slice it back underwater.

- Keep a respectful distance from animals such as moose, which have been known to charge canoeists.

- Use a zoom lens to get closeups; you'll be less intrusive.

- If parents or young animals get agitated, move farther away.

Nineteen years ago I walked the Barren Lands of northern Canada for the first time, and I was to return on four subsequent trips, lured by the vastness of the tundra. During my first morning I remember being brave and ambling solo about four miles along the spine of a sandy esker on Rennie Lake, until my senses began to overload. "There's a vibrant environment beneath the immediate desolation," I wrote in my journal. "Life is minute; it requires a look from many levels, from the top of the esker's highest point—where the breeze blows away the blackflies—to my knees, where I can discover tough, tiny flowers. Caribou bones are everywhere, bleached white and ghostly by the intensity of 24 hours of sunlight."

On that canoe trip I stood awestruck amid thousands of migrating caribou. Impressive as they were, I discovered that I am more fascinated by tundra wolves. My most memorable experience on the sandy Baillie River was *not* the Mama Grizz and her two cubs but the tundra wolves that cleverly tracked our fleet of canoes. Three lanky, grey wolves chased the stragglers in a small caribou herd, until our presence diverted them from an easy kill. They trotted downriver, keeping pace with our canoes, swam across the river, and disappeared into a nearby gully. About 15 minutes later my neck prickled, and I turned around to realize that the wolves had circled around to track us from behind, disguising their intent with a neat fake into the gully. Direct eye contact with the yellowish-green eyes of a wolf, I discovered, is a riveting experience.

They bolted for the ridge, and we stopped in the shadow of a sandy bank to watch them on the hillside. They howled to each other, the chorus of yips and yodels traveling though crisp, cold air. Peering over the top with binoculars, we saw the original three call in their family members, until six wolves appeared like sentinels at regular intervals along an esker. We returned to the canoes, drifting quietly downriver as the howls faded away on the wind.

Wildlife watching doesn't require an exotic location. You can find excitement at places close to home. My father and husband were fishing from their canoe at the mouth of the Androscoggin River near Maine's Umbagog Lake, right around the corner from an eagle's nest. They felt a presence over their shoulders and looked up to find an eagle closely watching their efforts. When my father unhooked a small fish that slithered away in the river, he heard the beat of heavy wings nearby and watched the eagle hook the fish in his talons. Four feet from the canoe. They started to cast repeatedly, hoping for more strikes. The eagle landed two more times to catch their rejects and an osprey dove once. It was the most profound wildlife experience they have had. It happened right around the corner from where I practically paddled under the legs of a moose munching plants in the twilight. For us, canoeing is the means to Close Encounters of the Animal Kind.

Chapter 11

RESOURCES

Once you begin canoeing, you can find a wealth of helpful resources to continue exploring the sport. Books, videos, magazines, and canoeing events can continue to excite you about many paddling possibilities and provide an excellent introduction to a variation on basic canoeing. I've included a variety of sources that have been particularly helpful or enjoyable to me.

The best overall source book is *The Whole Paddler's Catalog* by Zip Kellogg. Do not expect to find dry reading here. Zip includes his wry, colorful commentary on the sources, which makes the book an enjoyable excursion in its own right.

BOOKS

General Paddling

Bechdel, Les, and Slim Ray. 3d ed. *River Rescue: A Manual for Whitewater Safety.* Boston: Appalachian Mountain Club Books, 1997.

Gullion, Laurie. *Canoeing and Kayaking Instruction Manual.* Springfield, VA: American Canoe Association, 1994.

Kellogg, Zip, ed. *The Whole Paddler's Catalog.* Camden, ME: Ragged Mountain Press, 1997.

Lessels, Bruce. *Whitewater Handbook: Whitewater Kayaking and Canoeing from Beginner to Advanced.* Boston: Appalachian Mountain Club Books, 1994.

Walbridge, Charlie, and Wayne Sundmacher Sr. *Whitewater Rescue Manual: New Techniques for Canoeists, Kayakers, and Rafters.* Camden, ME: Ragged Mountain Press, 1995.

Webre, Anne Wortham, and Janet Zeller. *Canoeing and Kayaking Instruction Manual for Persons with Physical Disabilities.* Newington, VA: American Canoe Association, 1990.

Coffee Table Paddling

Crump, Donald J. *America's Wild and Scenic Rivers.* Washington, DC: National Geographic Society, 1983.

Jenkinson, Michael. *Wilderness Rivers of America.* Abrams, 1983 (currently out of print).

Raffan, James, ed. *Wild Waters: Canoeing North America's Wilderness Rivers.* Buffalo, NY: Firefly Books, 1997.

Other How-To-Canoe Books

Bell, Patricia. *Roughing It Elegantly: A Practical Guide to Canoe Camping.* Florence, OR: Cat's Paw Press, 1994.

Conover, Garrett. *Beyond the Paddle—A Canoeist's Guide to Expedition Skills: Poling, Lining, Portaging, and Maneuvering through the Ice.* Gardiner, ME: Tilbury House, 1991.

Davidson, James West, and John Rugge. *The Complete Wilderness Paddler.* New York: Vintage Books, 1983.

Foster, Thomas, and Kel Kelly. *Catch Every Eddy . . . Surf Every Wave: A Contemporary Guide to Whitewater Playboating.* Billerica, MA: Outdoor Center of New England, 1995.

Getchell, Annie. *The Essential Outdoor Gear Manual: Equipment Care and Repair for Outdoorspeople.* Camden, ME: Ragged Mountain Press, 1995.

Glaros, Lou. *Freestyle Canoeing: Contemporary Paddling Technique.* Birmingham, AL: Menasha Ridge Press, 1993.

Gullion, Laurie. *Canoeing (Outdoor Pursuits).* Champaign, IL: Human Kinetics, 1993.

Heed, Peter and Dick Mansfield. *Canoe Racing: The Competitor's Guide to Marathon and Downriver Canoe Racing.* Springfield, IL: Acorn Publishing, 1992.

Jacobson, Clif. *Canoe and Camping: Beyond the Basics.* Merrillville, IN: ICS Books, 1995.

Rock, Harry. *The Basic Essentials of Canoe Poling.* Merrillville, IN: ICS Books, 1992.

Canoeing for the Soul

Kimber, Robert. *The Canoeist's Sketchbook.* White River Junction, VT: Chelsea Green Publishing, 1991.

Mason, Bill, and Paul Mason. *Path of the Paddle.* Revised and updated ed. Minocqua, WI: NorthWord Press, 1995.

Mason, Bill. *Song of the Paddle: An Illustrated Guide to Wilderness Camping.* Buffalo, NY: Key Porter Books, 1997.

Women's History

Aspen, Jean. *Arctic Daughter: A Wilderness Journey.* Minneapolis: Bergamot Books, 1988 (currently out of print).

Cameron, Agnes Deans. *The New North: An Account of a Woman's 1908 Journey through Canada to the Arctic.* Western Producer Prairie Books, 1986 (currently out of print).

Davidson, James West, John Rugge, and Philip Turner (editor). *Great Heart: The History of a Labrador Adventure.* New York: Kodansha, 1997.

Fons, Valerie. *Keep It Moving: Baja by Canoe.* Seattle: The Mountaineers, 1986 (currently out of print).

Helmericks, Constance. *Down the Wild River North.* Minneapolis: Bergamot Books, 1989 edition (currently out of print).

Hubbard, Mina. *A Woman's Way through Unknown Labrador: An Account of the Exploration of the Nascaupee and George Rivers.* Temecula, CA: Reprint Services Corp./American Biography Service, 1991.

Kerfoot, Justine. *Woman of the Boundary Waters: Canoeing, Guiding, Mushing, and Surviving.* Reprint ed. Minneapolis: University of Minnesota Press, 1994.

Murie, Margaret. *Two in the Far North.* 35th anniversary ed. Seattle: Alaska Northwest Publishing, 1997.

Neimi, Judith, and Barbara Wieser, eds. *Rivers Running Free: Canoeing Stories by Adventurous Women.* Seattle: Seal Press, 1992.

General History

Hodgins, Bruce W., and Margaret Hobbs (editor). *Nastawgan: The Canadian North by Canoe and Snowshoe.* Betelgeuse Books, 1987.

MacGregor, John. *A Thousand Miles in the Rob Roy Canoe on Rivers and Lakes of Europe.* British Canoe Union, 1963 edition.

Vine, P. A. L. *Pleasure Boating in the Victorian Era: An Anthology of Some of the More Enterprising Voyages Made in Pleasure Boats on Inland Waterways during the Nineteenth Century.* Phillimore & Co., 1983 (currently out of print).

Canoeing with Kids

Gordon, Herb. *The Joy of Family Camping.* Burford Books, 1998.

Gullion, Laurie. *The American Canoe Association's Kayak and Canoe Games.* Birmingham, AL: Menasha Ridge Press, 1996.

Shears, Nick. *Paddle America: A Guide to Trips and Outfitters in All 50 States.* 3d ed. Washington, DC: Starfish Press, 1996.

Shepardson, Carl and Marge. *The Family Canoe Trip: A Unique Approach to Family Canoeing.* Merrillville, IN: ICS Books, 1985.

Ethics

Meyer, Kathleen. *How to Shit in the Woods: An Environmentally Sound Approach to a Lost Art.* 2d ed. Berkeley: Ten Speed Press, 1994.

Cooking

Daniel, Linda. *Camp Cookery: A Handbook of Provisions and Recipes.* Old Saybrook, CT: Globe Pequot Press, 1988.

Latimer, Carole. *Wilderness Cuisine: How to Prepare and Enjoy Fine Food on the Trail and in Camp.* Berkeley: Wilderness Press, 1991.

McCairen, Patricia. *River Runners' Recipes.* Spiral ed. Birmingham, AL: Menasha Ridge Press, 1997.

Miller, Dorcas. *Good Food for Camp and Trail: All-Natural Recipes for Delicious Meals Outdoors.* Boulder: Pruett Publishing, 1993.

National Outdoor Leadership School, and Claudia Pearson (editor). *NOLS Cookery.* 4th ed. Mechanicsburg, PA: Stackpole Books, 1997.

First Aid

Isaac, Jeffrey, and Peter Goth. *The Outward Bound Wilderness First-Aid Handbook.* 3d ed. Rockville, MD: Lyons Press, 1998.

Tilton, Buck, and Frank Hubbell. *Medicine for the Backcountry.* 2d ed. Merrillville, IN: ICS Books, 1994.

MAGAZINES AND NEWSLETTERS

American Rivers
1025 Vermont Ave., NW, Suite 720
Washington, DC 20005
Phone 202-347-7550
Fax 202-347-9240
www.amrivers.org

American Whitewater
P.O. Box 636
16 Bull Run
Margaretville, NY 12455
Phone 914-688-5569
www.awa.org

Canoe & Kayak
P.O. Box 3146
Kirkland, WA 98083
Phone 206-827-6363
Fax 425-827-1893
www.canoekayak.com

Hurley's Journal
6325-9 Falls of Neuse Road, #353
Raleigh, NC 27615-6809
Phone 919-872-2627
Fax 919-876-4564
E-mail: editor@hurleysjournal.com
www.hurleysjournal.com

Kanawa
Canadian Recreational Canoe Association
P.O. Box 398
446 Main Street West
Merrickville, ON K0G 1N0
Canada
Phone 888-252-6292
Fax 613-269-2908
www.crca.ca/kanawa.html

Paddler
Paddlesport Publishing, Inc.
P.O. Box 775450
Steamboat Springs, CO 80477
Phone 970-879-1450
www.aca.paddler.org

Wooden Canoe Journal
Wooden Canoe Heritage Association
P.O. Box 224
Cooperstown, NY 13326
Phone 607-547-2762
Fax 607-547-1223
E-mail: journal@wcha.org
www.wcha.org

OTHER ELECTRONIC RESOURCES

Adventurous Traveler Bookstore
(maps and regional guidebooks)
245 South Champlain
Burlington, VT 05401
Phone 800-282-3963
Fax 800-677-1821
E-mail: books@atbook.com
www.adventuroustraveler.com

GORP: Great Outdoor Recreation Pages
www.gorp.com

VIDEOS

Babes in the Woods: Extended Canoe Camping with Small Children by Northern Stars Planetarium
4 Osborne St.
Fairfield, ME 04937
Phone 207-453-7668

Cold, Wet & Alive by Nichols Production/American Canoe Association
7432 Alban Station Blvd., Suite B-226
Springfield, VA 22150
Phone 703-451-0141
Fax 703-451-2245
E-mail: acadirect@aol.com
www.aca-paddler.org

From Here to There by the Nantahala Outdoor Center staff
13077 Highway 19 West
Bryson City, NC 28713
Phone 704-488-2175
www.nocweb.com

Path of the Paddle: Whitewater by
Bill Mason
National Film Board of Canada
350 Fifth Ave., Suite 4820
New York, NY 10118
Phone 212-629-8890
Fax 212-629-8502
E-mail: j.sirabella@nfb.ca
www.nfb.ca:80/FMT/E/real/M/
   Mason_Bill.html

Path of the Paddle: Quietwater by
Bill Mason
National Film Board of Canada
350 Fifth Ave., Suite 4820
New York, NY 10118
Phone 212-629-8890
Fax 212-629-8502
E-mail: j.sirabella@nfb.ca
www.nfb.ca:80/FMT/E/real/M/
   Mason_Bill.html

Solo Playboating I by Kent Ford,
   Whitewater Instruction, Durango,
   CO
7432 Alban Station Blvd.
Suite B-226
Springfield, VA 22150
Phone 703-451-0141
Fax 703-451-2245
E-mail: acadirect@aol.com
www.aca-paddler.org

Solo Playboating II by Kent Ford,
   Whitewater Instruction, Durango,
   CO
7432 Alban Station Blvd.
Suite B-226
Springfield, VA 22150
Phone 703-451-0141
Fax 703-451-2245
E-mail: acadirect@aol.com
www.aca-paddler.org

Waterwalker by Bill Mason
National Film Board of Canada
350 Fifth Ave., Suite 4820
New York, NY 10118
Phone 212-629-8890
Fax 212-629-8502
E-mail: j.sirabella@nfb.ca
www.nfb.ca:80/FMT/E/real/M/
   Mason_Bill.html).

National Organizations

American Canoe Association
7432 Alban Station Blvd.
Suite B-226
Springfield, VA 22150
Phone 703-451-0141
Fax 703-451-2245
E-mail: acadirect@aol.com
www.aca-paddler.org

American Rivers
1025 Vermont Ave., NW, Suite 720
Washington, DC 20005
Phone 202-347-7550
Fax 202-347-9240
www.amrivers.org

American Whitewater
P.O. Box 636
16 Bull Run Road
Margaretville, NY 12455
Phone/Fax 914-586-3050
www.awa.org

Canadian Recreational Canoe
   Association
P.O. Box 398
446 Main Street West
Merrickville, ON K0G 1N0
Canada
Phone 888-252-6292
Fax 613-269-2908
E-mail: staff@crca.ca
www.crca.ca

Professional Paddlesports
   Association
P.O. Box 248
Butler, KY 41006
Phone 606-472-2205
www.propaddle.com

Local clubs

Contact American Canoe
Association or the American
Whitewater Affiliation for member
lists.

Adirondack Mountain Club
814 Goggins Road
Lake George, NY 12845-4117
Phone 800-395-8080
Fax 518-668-3746
E-mail: adkinfo@adk.org
www.adk.org

Appalachian Mountain Club
5 Joy Street
Boston, MA 02108
Phone 617-523-0636
www.outdoors.org

GENERAL OUTDOOR COURSES
AND NETWORKING

Becoming an Outdoors-Woman
Dr. Christine Thomas
College of Natural Resources
University of Wisconsin–Stevens
   Point
Stevens Point, WI 54481
Phone 877-BOWOMAN
E-mail: cthomas@uwsp.edu
www1.uwsp.edu/general/commun/
   bow/index.htm

L.L. Bean Outdoor Discovery
   Schools
15 Casco Street
Freeport, ME 04033
Phone 888-552-3261
Email: outdoor.discovery.com
www.llbean.com/odp

National Outdoor Leadership
   School
288 Main Street
Lander, WY 82520
Phone 307-332-6973
Phone for Leave No Trace
   800-332-4100
Fax 307-332-1220
E-mail: admissions@nols.edu
www.nols.edu

Women's Outdoor Network
P.O. Box 50003
Palo Alto, CA 94303

Women's Sports Foundation
Eisenhower Park
East Meadow, NY 11554
Phone 800-227-3988, 516-542-4700
Fax 516-542-4716
E-mail: WoSport@aol.com
www.lifetimetv.com/WoSport

OUTFITTERS FOR WOMEN

Classic Solo Canoeing
Becky Mason
P.O. Box 126, RR #1
Chelsea, PQ J0X 1N0
Canada
Phone 819-827-4159
E-mail: redcanoe@istar.ca
www.wilds.mb.ca/redcanoe

Explorations in Travel
1922 River Road
Guilford, VT 05301
Phone 802-257-0152

**Outdoor Vacations for
  Women Over 40**
Groton, MA
Phone 978-448-3331

Women in the Wilderness
566 Ottawa Ave.
St. Paul, MN 55107-2550
Phone 651-227-2284
Fax 651-227-4028

Woodswomen
25 West Diamond Lake Road
Minneapolis, MN 55419-1926
Phone 800-279-0555
Fax 612-822-3814
www.woodswomen.mn.org

WOMEN'S WELLNESS

The Melpomene Institute
1010 University Avenue
St. Paul, MN 55104
Phone 612-642-1951
Fax 612-642-1871
E-mail: melpomen@skypoint.com
www.melpomene.org

Index

··

"This new series is designed to teach outdoor skills
to women in the way they learn. . . . Women of all
ages describe how they overcame obstacles, what
they enjoyed most, or just how they felt about
undertaking a new activity . . . extremely well
done and appealing."

··